ET TU, BRUTE?

ET TU, BRUTE?

The Best Latin Lines Ever

Harry Mount and John Davie

BLOOMSBURY CONTINUUM
LONDON • OXFORD • NEW YORK • NEW DELHI • SYDNEY

BLOOMSBURY CONTINUUM
Bloomsbury Publishing Plc
50 Bedford Square, London, WC1B 3DP, UK
29 Earlsfort Terrace, Dublin 2, Ireland

BLOOMSBURY, BLOOMSBURY CONTINUUM and the Diana logo are trademarks of Bloomsbury Publishing Plc

First published in Great Britain 2022

A catalogue record for this book is available from the British Library

Library of Congress Cataloguing-in-Publication data has been applied for

ISBN: HB: 978-1-3994-0097-8; eBook: 978-1-3994-0099-2;
ePDF: 978-1-3994-0101-2

6 8 10 9 7 5

Typeset by Deanta Global Publishing Services, Chennai, India
Printed and bound in Great Britain by CPI Group (UK) Ltd, Croydon CR0 4YY

In Memoriam Lindy Dufferin (1941–2020) and
Jasper Griffin (1937–2019)

CONTENTS

INTRODUCTION

The word of the decade – here's hoping it isn't the word of the century – is a Latin hybrid.

Coronavirus comes from the Latin **corona**, meaning **crown**, and the Latin **virus**, originally meaning **a poisonous secretion from snakes** – i.e. a kind of venom. Scientists gave the virus the name because those knobbly bits on the surface of the virus are like the crests and balls of a crown. In Latin, **corona** originally meant **a wreath of flowers** or, sometimes, of precious metals. You see these delicate golden wreaths of flowers across the ancient world, in Greece and Rome.

The Latin word *corona* is derived from the Greek word *korone*. In time, the word *corona* was used of all crowns, whether floral or not. Our word crown comes from *corona*. Crowns – or *coronae* – were worn in the ancient world by kings and placed on statues of the gods as offerings. In a mocking way, *coronae* were put on slaves' heads, too, when they went up for auction. They were even worn as a cure for headaches.

Virus is also a Latin word, originally derived from the Greek *ios*. As well as meaning a poisonous secretion by snakes, it was also used in Latin to mean a poisonous emanation from a plant, a poisonous fluid, a nasty manner of speech or disposition, an acrid juice or a magic potion. Used together, though, the words corona and virus these days have only one miserable meaning.

Once again, even with the worst of modern horrors, it is the Latin language that put it first and put it best – unless ancient

Greek got there first, by lending its alphabet to those horrible virus variants like Delta and Omicron. This book will help you understand the Latin words, like coronavirus, that are still all around us today.

Latin lives on in some corners of Britain – even where it shouldn't. Justin Warshaw QC, a family lawyer, still finds Latin useful today in his work:

> The law is a goldmine of great Latin tags. Legal Latin was apparently abolished by Lord Woolf in 1999, acting *pro bono*. Thankfully the judgment was *interim* and, *mutatis mutandis*, major reforms have been avoided. The forum is still *conveniens*, the *locus* is still *in quo*, the *amicus curiae* is still briefed, *habeas corpus* invoked, a judge can be *functus*, legitimate reductions remain *pro tanto*, the Carta remains Magna, the guilty has *mens rea* for his *actus reus* and adjournments can still be *sine die*.

All these legal terms are explained in the glossary of Latin words in English at the back of this book, by the way. It is an updated version of the Latin phrase book in Harry Mount's *Amo, Amas, Amat … and All That* (2006).

And there still is plenty of Latin left in everyday, non-legal life, even if some people want to get rid of it. As Charles Moore wrote in the *Spectator* on 29 May 2021:

> O tempora, o mores. A worried report from the Social Mobility Commission claimed last week that many top civil servants know Latin, and use it, thereby excluding their less privileged colleagues.
>
> I am trying to help stamp this practice out by constructing a lingua franca purged of hard-to-understand terms

> from the snobby old Romans e.g. (exempli gratia) circus, video, doctor, bonus, exit, femur, stet, quantum, trans, memorandum, focus, alumnus, camera, conductor, radius, maximum, minimum, major, minor, senior, junior, media, gratis, post-mortem, ego, versus, data, species, penis and vagina, i.e. (id est) quite a lot of words.
>
> It is hard work, but we must jettison stuffy old concepts like habeas corpus, pro bono, sub judice, de jure, de facto and de minimis non curat lex – all so twentieth-century.
>
> Then there are all those initials. AD is now on the way out, but why must we make people uncomfortable by using a.m./p.m. (ante and post meridiem) to tell the time, and how dare the Queen call her herself DG Reg FD on our coinage?
>
> It must, a fortiori, be intimidating for would-be civil servants from deprived backgrounds to have to wrestle with a CV (curriculum vitae), and ipso facto, become persona non grata. Res ipsa loquitur, QED (quod erat demonstrandum), etc. (et cetera). Latin: RIP (requiescat in pace). When levelling up, it is much better to use good old English words like hoi polloi.

Again, you'll find the Latin words Charles Moore mentions in this book's glossary. A lot of them have become English words used by everyone – like 'senior' and 'junior'. Charles Moore might also have included the Latin word **spectator**. It means exactly the same in Latin as in English – and it also happens to be the name of the magazine he wrote these words in.

We rarely stop to think what extraordinary survivals they are: completely intact words transported all the way from ancient Rome, unsullied by a journey across a continent and several millennia.

Other Latin phrases, though, once in more regular use – like '*a fortiori*' – are in decline. This book aims to reverse that decline. How sad it would be if those pure Latin words disappeared from the English language – even if we'll always have Latin- and Greek-inspired words.

As well as defining Latin words used in English, this book principally shows how the Romans really looked at the world in their native language: how they looked at love, sex, politics and everyday life. Latin isn't an austere relic to be worshipped behind glass, at a distance, in a museum. Latin is there to make you laugh, move you to tears, and charm you by its beauty and cleverness. But by its pleasing cleverness, not its scary cleverness.

That pleasing cleverness is why people still drop Latin into their speeches to add a little extra heft. The Queen did it in her speech at the Guildhall on 24 November 1992. Windsor Castle had just burned down. Princess Anne had divorced. The marriage of Charles and Diana was crumbling and Prince Andrew had separated from Fergie – who had just had her toe sucked by the American financier John Bryan. That's why the Queen declared: 'In the words of one of my more sympathetic correspondents, it has turned out to be an annus horribilis.'

Elizabeth II's ancestor Elizabeth I was even keener on the Latin language.

Amazingly, her Latin handwriting survives. She was extremely good at the subject, translating *The Consolation of Philosophy* by Boethius into English and correcting her little brother Edward's (as in Edward VI) Latin exercises. The Queen's motto was a charmingly simple one:

Semper eadem.

Always the same.

Other royal mottoes include:

Nemo me impune lacessit.

No one provokes me with impunity.

Motto of the Crown of Scotland and all Scottish regiments

A 2021 exhibition, *Love's Labour's Found*, at the Philip Mould Gallery in London, showed how obsessed the Tudors were with Latin. An anonymous Edward VI portrait in the show had these words written around the frame:

EDWARDI SEXTI ANGLIE, FRNCIE ET HIBERNICE REGIS VERA EFFIGIES EO PRIMU TEMPORE QUO REGIA CORONA EST INSIGNITUS AETATIS SUE 10 ANO 1547.

Edward VI gets his Latin wrong.

Gratifyingly, there are a few mistakes there – notably *primu*, which should be *primo*. But the meaning is still clear: **A true**

effigy of Edward VI, King of England, France and Ireland, at the first moment the royal crown was placed upon him, at the age of ten, in 1547.

The Latin – harder to read – on another portrait, of William Arundell by George Gower, says, **Non spirat qui non aspirat – He who doesn't aspire doesn't breathe.** Arundell's motto is a nice play on the Cicero line, **Dum spiro spero – While I breathe, I hope.**

Ciceronian – William Arundell by George Gower (1580).

Up in the top left corner, the Latin reads, **Ano Dni 1580, atatis sua 20 – In the year of God 1580, at the age of 20.** Again, there's another mistake there – it should be 'aetatis'.

In a funny way, those mistakes actually show how familiar with Latin the Tudors were. Just like people making spelling mistakes in English today, because they don't bother to check a familiar language, these Tudor painters were familiar enough with Latin to write it badly, rather than checking with a scholarly figure before they wrote their words.

It wasn't just in sixteenth-century England that Latin was so popular. Across Europe in the Middle Ages, Latin was the intellectual **lingua franca** (a bridge language or **Frankish language** – as in the Franks, the word used for Western Europeans in the late Byzantine Empire). So William of Ockham (a village in Surrey) used Latin for his famous rule

Entia non sunt multiplicanda praeter necessitatem.

No more things should be presumed to exist than are absolutely necessary.

The principle of Occam's Razor, named after William of Occam (1285–1349): that simpler explanations are better than complicated ones.

300 years later, the French philosopher René Descartes (1596–1650) was using Latin for his principle,

Cogito, ergo sum.

I think, therefore I am.

Discourse on the Method, 1637

This line was a crucial building block in Western philosophy, as a basic proof of thought and knowledge. Most thoughts and knowledge might be imaginary, but the very fact of a thought means there must be a thinking entity.

Also in France, a little earlier, the philosopher Michel de Montaigne (1533–92) was a Latin obsessive, as was his father, who wanted his son to have Latin as his first language. In his father's Bordeaux chateau, servants were ordered to speak to little Montaigne in Latin only, as both his mother and father did. It worked. Montaigne became fluent in Latin and even had Latin and Greek quotes painted on the roof beams of his library for inspiration. Among them was this one:

Solum certum nihil esse certi
et homine miserius aut superbius.

Only one thing is certain: that nothing is certain – and nothing is more sad or arrogant than man.

Pliny the Elder, *Natural History* II, 7

Enoch Powell, a Greek Professor at Sydney University at the age of 25, turned to Latin, too, for his – *horribilis* – 1968 'Rivers of Blood' speech. When he declared, 'Like the Roman, I seem to see "the River Tiber foaming with much blood",' he was quoting Virgil. He was referring to the passage in *The Aeneid* where the Cumaean Sibyl predicted to Aeneas that a war in Italy would make the River Tiber run red with the victims' blood.

Bella, horrida bella,
Et Thybrim multo spumantem sanguine cerno.

I see wars, horrible wars and the Tiber foaming with much blood.

The Aeneid, 6.86–7

In *Withnail & I* (1987), Withnail (Richard E. Grant) and Uncle Monty (Richard Griffiths) also use Latin to add spice to their drunken game of poker. They alienate Marwood (Paul McGann) by speaking in Latin:

Uncle Monty: **Nonne solus cedetur? [Surely, only Marwood will lose.]**

Withnail: **Reginae servandae defit. [He's short of the queen that can save him.]**

[Uncle Monty giggles at the idea of a queen coming to the rescue]

For all the high-minded pleasure these little bursts of Latin give when they're dropped into English, the Romans didn't think it was such a high-falutin' language. As the first chapter in this book, on Roman graffiti, shows, Latin was used in the most wonderfully vulgar, low-falutin' way. Take this graffiti found at Pompeii:

Lucilla ex corpore lucrum faciebat.

Lucilla made money from her body.

You can't get much more direct than that.

Because the teaching of Latin, so unfairly, has been increasingly restricted to private schools and grammar schools, it's wrongly thought of as a 'posh' language. That impression is deepened by Latin's use in mottoes and for inscriptions on grand buildings.

But, as that Roman graffiti shows, people swore in Latin; they haggled with prostitutes in Latin; launderers wrote their laundry signs in Latin. And, also, some of the finest poetry ever written has been in Latin. That's here, too: in small chunks in the original Latin, with English translations, and a reference – so you can find the full poem, either in print or online.

The references are done in the conventional way. So *Epp.* 2.2.55 means Horace's Epistles, Book 2, Epistle number 2 and line 55.

A lot of Latin's best lines will be familiar to you but the context might not be, like this one.

Festina lente.

Make haste slowly.

Suetonius on Augustus, *Lives of the Caesars*, 25

In other words, if you want to get things done quickly, do them slowly. Suetonius applied the concept to Augustus, who very slowly turned Rome from a republic to an empire, with none of the chaos that would have come of doing it quickly. Or take the Juvenal line:

Quis custodiet ipsos custodes?

Who will guard the guards themselves?

Satires, 6.346–8

This quotation is often used as a moral warning against politicians and the Establishment and the potential for corruption. In fact, Juvenal was writing about stopping a wife from sleeping with her guards.

Audio quid veteres olim moneatis amici, 'Pone seram, cohibe.' Sed quis custodiet ipsos custodes? Cauta est et ab illis incipit uxor.

I hear what my old friends warn me: 'Bolt her in. Constrain her!' But who will guard her guards themselves? My wife plans ahead and starts with the guards.

Satires, 6.346–8

Quis custodiet ipsos custodes has since found its way into pretty regular English usage. Juvenal had plenty more lines that aren't found in English, but should be:

Rara est adeo concordia formae atque pudicitiae.

So rarely do good looks and good behaviour go together.

Satires, 10.297–8

Mors sola fatetur quantula sint hominum corpuscula.

Only death reveals the tiny dimensions of our human frame.

Satires, 10.172–3

Desperanda tibi salva concordia socru.

Abandon any hope of a peaceful existence if your mother-in-law is alive.

Satires, 6.231

In this book, you'll find sentiments you've heard in English but might not know are translations from Latin:

Audentis Fortuna iuvat.

Fortune favours the brave.

Virgil, *Aeneid*, 10.284

Or what about this familiar line, also from Virgil?

Sed fugit interea, fugit inreparabile tempus.

But, meanwhile, irretrievable time is slipping away.

Georgics, 3.284, often shortened to '*Tempus fugit*' – Time flies

Roman views of life often seem astonishingly modern. Take Horace's opinion on travel:

Caelum, non animum, mutant qui trans mare currunt.

Men change the sky over their heads, not their state of mind, when they dash off overseas.

Horace, *Epistles*, 1.11.27

Or Horace's opinion of those vain enterprises we like to think of as earth-shatteringly important:

Parturient montes, nascetur ridiculus mus.

Mountains will go into labour and a silly little mouse will be born.

Horace, *Ars Poetica*, 139

And has anyone ever summed up egomania quite so well as Catullus?

Desine de quoquam quicquam bene velle mereri aut aliquem fieri posse putare pium.

Stop wanting to deserve any thanks from anyone, or thinking that anybody can be grateful.

Catullus, *Carmina*, 73

Then there are those moments when the ancient Roman reaches out from the page and points out something you thought you'd come up with yourself only a moment ago:

Nemo enim fere saltat sobrius, nisi forte insaniter.

Hardly anyone dances sober, unless they're quite mad.

Cicero, *Pro Murena*, 1.13

Medicus enim nihil aliud est quam animi consolatio.

You see, a doctor's nothing more than a vehicle for consolation.

Petronius, *Satyricon* 42

People think of Latin as being a tremendously pompous, grandiloquent (***grandis*** – **grand**; ***loquens*** – **speaking**) language. They often think of it, too, as a technocratic language, because Latinate words are used for scientific, medical or technical terms in English. Or architectural ones. Take Vitruvius (*c.* 80–15 BC), the first great architectural historian, author of ***De Architectura*** (**About Architecture**). Here he lays out his three principles for buildings:

> **Haec autem ita fieri debent, ut habeatur ratio firmitatis, utilitatis, venustatis.**
>
> **Now these should be done so that account is taken of strength, usefulness and grace.**
>
> Vitruvius, *De Architectura*

If you translated those three principles into their nearest English equivalents, they *would* sound pretty pompous: firmity, utility and 'Venusness'. But that's only because, in English, we prefer Anglo-Saxon words for directness and simplicity, not least in swear words.

And so we have become wary of using long, Latinate words in English.

In the original Latin, that doesn't apply. In fact, paradoxically, Latin's beauty lies in its concision and pithiness. Very often you'll see in this book how a short Latin expression requires a longer, less romantic and more windily explicit translation in English. So these two words by Cicero are the quickest way to ask who's getting the best of the deal:

> **Cui bono?**
>
> **To whose benefit?**
>
> Cicero, quoting the jurist Cassius Longinus, *Pro Milone*, 12.32

Look at Ovid's wonderfully brief piece of advice, sadly not taken by the Duke of York:

Ut ameris, amabilis esto.

If you want people to like you, be likeable.

Or take the beautifully concise expression **sub specie aeternitatis – under the appearance of eternity**. Coined by the Dutch philosopher Baruch Spinoza (1632–77), the expression means something like 'viewed from the perspective of eternity'. It's hard to translate it into English without coming up with something rather cumbersome and nebulous. The original Latin is crystal clear – and very short.

No wonder Latin came to be used for mottoes and witticisms. The shorter and more crammed with meaning an idea is, the more memorable it becomes, as Virgil shows:

Dux femina facti.

The leader of the venture was a woman.

Aeneid, 1.364

At this point in *The Aeneid*, Venus is explaining to her son, Aeneas, how Dido, Aeneas's future lover, became Queen of Carthage. But those three short words – *Dux femina facti* – have become shorthand for praising, or damning, women engaged on any enterprise.

The same compression principle applies to spells in Latin, as J. K. Rowling shrewdly worked out. Individual Latin words may be complex but, because they mean so much, just a few of them carry a lot of weight. Take a look at the spells from the Harry Potter books, often written in Rowling's charming, made-up Latin – always beautifully concise:

HARRY POTTER'S LATIN SPELLS

Accio – Summon! (From **accio – I summon**.)

Confundo – Confound! (From **confundo – I confound**.)

Crucio – I torture you. (From **crucio – I torture**.)

Expecto Patronum – I await a protector. (From **exspecto – I await** – and **patronus** – **patron** or **protector**.)

Expelliarmus – Disarm. (A made-up word, inspired by **expello – I expel** – and **arma – weapons**.)

Finite Incantatum – Finish the spell.

Imperio – I control you. (A made-up word, inspired by **impero – I command**.)

Lumos – light. (Another made-up word, derived from **lumen – light**.)

Nox **– night**.

Obliviate – Forget. (A made-up word, derived from **obliviscor – I forget**.)

Petrificus totalus – turn completely to stone. (New words, derived from **petra – rock** – and **facio – I make** – and **totus – whole**.)

Riddikulus – laughable. (A made-up word, based on **ridiculus – funny** – from where we get '**ridiculous**'.)

Sectumsempra – Keep on slashing. (A made-up word, derived from **seco – I cut** – and **semper – always**.)

Stupefy – the same as the English word. (Derived from **stupefacio – I stupefy**.)

As a fan of Latin, J. K. Rowling also coined the appealingly concise motto for Hogwarts School of Witchcraft and Wizardry:

Draco Dormiens Nunquam Titillandus.

Never tickle a sleeping dragon.

Again and again, you'll find the most memorable Latin lines are the shortest ones, from Horace's

Nunc est bibendum.

Now we must drink

to

Alea iacta est.

The die is cast.

This was said by Caesar as he crossed the Rubicon river, just north of modern Rimini, in 49 BC in his battle with Pompey. By crossing the river that separated Cisalpine Gaul from Rome, Caesar reached the point of no going back, where war was inevitable.

Caesar was responsible, of course, for the most famous – and shortest – of all Latin lines:

Veni, vidi, vici.

I came, I saw, I conquered.

Plutarch's *Life of Caesar*, 50.2

He said the line after his victory over Pharnaces II, King of Pontus, at Zela, now in Turkey, in 47 BC.

In this book, you'll find short extracts from poems, from Horace's **Carpe diem** to **Arma virumque cano**, the first line of Virgil's *Aeneid*. Then there are longer extracts – like Cicero's tips for dealing with old age. He mainly recommended taking up a hobby: 'I'm 62 and I'm learning Greek. I love it. I drink it down greedily like I'm satisfying a long-standing thirst. Socrates learned how to play the lyre in old age.'

And, for tips on how to deal with life's misfortunes at any age, here is Seneca:

Non quid sed quemadmodum feras interest.

It is not what you endure that matters, but how you endure it.

The ***corpus*** (**body**) of classical and medieval Latin literature and inscriptions is so vast that only the tip of the iceberg can squeeze between these covers. But we hope that, through this moving, funny collection of brainy prose, salacious graffiti and often very rude poetry, any reader – whether a Latin lover or not, to begin with – will get an instant hit of real life in ancient Rome and the Roman Empire: in the brothels and legionaries' camps, as well as in the emperors' palaces and at the poets' symposia.

This is Rome as the Romans saw, spoke and wrote about it.

A NOTE ON TRANSLATION

Throughout the book, we have highlighted both the Latin expression and its English translation in bold:

> **Otium sine litteris mors est et hominis vivi sepultura.**
>
> **Leisure without study is death and a tomb for a man who's alive.**
>
> Seneca, *Letter to Lucilius*, 82

This is so you can easily pick out the Latin lines and their translation – and make out the similarities between the Latin and the English. You won't need to have studied Latin to see those similarities. Two thirds of English words come from Latin or Greek. So there are a lot of echoes you'll recognize.

The main reason why two thirds of English words derive from Latin and, to a lesser extent, Greek is the Norman invasion of 1066. The law, politics, the church and education were all represented by Normans, whose language was strongly Latinate. Anglo-Saxons, who tended to be poorer, continued to speak Anglo-Saxon, but the upper echelons of society spoke Norman French, which was strongly underpinned by Latin.

So, even today, many people will use 'get' but may not understand the Latinate synonyms 'obtain/procure/acquire'. That's the main reason why any English literature written before 1900, packed as it is with more complicated Latinate words, is a closed shop to lots of people – unless they're lucky enough to have done Latin!

Admittedly, plenty of those Latinate words aren't used much any more. We all know what senile, virile, juvenile and puerile mean, but you won't hear these related words every day:

> Puellile – like a girl (from **puella – girl**)
>
> Muliebrile – like a woman (from **mulier – woman**)
>
> Anile – like an old woman (from **anus – old woman**. NB: different from the other sort of anus, which derives from the Latin for 'ring' or 'circle')

But, with a basic knowledge of Latin, these lost, English, Latinate words spring to life. You don't need to have learnt Latin to be able to recognize its legacy in the English language. Once you identify the general principles of Latinate words, you'll be able to trace individual similarities between English words and their Latin ancestors. As Cato the Elder advised trainee lawyers,

> **Rem tene, verba sequentur.**
>
> **Grasp the case – the words will follow.**

To see how often English words emerge naturally out of the Latin, look at Horace's most famous quotation, from where we get the expression **Carpe diem – Seize the day**:

> **Dum loquimur, fugerit invida aetas; carpe diem, quam minimum credula postero.**
>
> **While we've been speaking, envious time has fled; seize the day, and place no trust in tomorrow.**
>
> *Odes*, 1.11.7–8

There are lots of words in the Latin that chime with the English translation: **loquimur**, as in loquacious, means **we speak. Fugerit**, as in fugitive, means **has fled**.

Beware, though: lots of English words look very like Latin words, but aren't always derived from the most obvious Latin word you can think of. Take the word 'celebrity'. It comes from **celeber**, meaning **famous** – not to be confused with **caelebs** or **coelebs**, meaning **single**, which gives us the word celibate. The Latin name for the chaffinch is **Fringilla coelebs** – the **bachelor bird**, because it often flocks in all-male groups.

With the quotations and the translations in this book in bold, it means you can, if you want, just pick out the Latin, and the English translations, to hear about Rome straight from the horse's mouth, without reading the commentary in between.

You will soon start to see resemblances between different words with the same core. So these two expressions both come from **caveo – I beware of**:

Caveat emptor.

Let the buyer beware.

Cave canem.

Beware of the dog.

(The latter is found on a famous mosaic of a dog on a front doorstep in Pompeii)

Most of the Latin quotations in this book are one- or two-liners. There are longer passages, such as Tacitus on how unsophisticated ancient Britons were, or Cicero on old age. But these longer passages are mostly in English, with a few key words translated into Latin.

We can't know, by the way, exactly how Latin was pronounced. But there are some clues. Proof for the Romans pronouncing a 'v' as a 'w' comes in Cicero.

He describes how, after Caesar crossed the Rubicon in 49 BC (see page 16), his troops marched on Rome so fast that his enemy, Pompey, just had time to leave Italy for Greece.

As Pompey's ship was in the port of Dyrrachium, a man was noisily advertising his figs on the quay. He was shouting, 'Cauneas!' – short for **Cauneas ficos vendo (I'm selling figs from Cauneae)**. An officer told Pompey the man was warning him not to leave port. He had misunderstood the words in the hawker's cry to say, **Cave ne eas! – Beware of leaving!**

The confusion would only have happened if the 'v' of 'Cave' sounded like a 'w'.

Finally, bear in mind that this isn't a teach-yourself-Latin book. But we hope you get pleasure in seeing the thousands of similarities between English and Latin. And when you do see one, almost always it's because the English word grew out of the Latin one. Spotting those links is a great delight.

As St Augustine said, now there is nothing to do but

Tolle lege, tolle lege.

Take up and read, take up and read.

St Augustine, *Confessions*, 8.12

A TIMELINE OF JULIUS CAESAR AND THE ROMAN EMPERORS

ROMULUS AND REMUS were twin brothers. According to legend, Romulus founded Rome, the city named after him, in 753 BC after killing Remus. Remus had mocked Romulus by jumping over Romulus's first flimsy walls around Rome.

Romulus and Remus were the twin sons of Rhea Silvia by the god Mars. When their mother was imprisoned by their wicked great-uncle, the twins were saved and suckled by a she-wolf.

After Romulus, the kings of Rome lasted until the Roman Republic began in 509 BC.

The ROMAN REPUBLIC lasted from the overthrow of the Roman Kingdom in 509 BC to the moment Augustus became the first emperor in 27 BC.

JULIUS CAESAR (100–44 BC): Dictator of Rome from 49 BC until his assassination on the Ides of March (15 March), 44 BC.

AUGUSTUS (63 BC–14 AD) ruled from 27 BC to 14 AD.

TIBERIUS ruled 14–37 AD.

GAIUS (Caligula) ruled 37–41 AD.

CLAUDIUS ruled 41–54 AD.

NERO (last of the Julio–Claudian dynasty) ruled 54–68 AD.

GALBA, OTHO, VITELLIUS ruled 68–9 AD. (A year of civil war followed Nero's death without an heir, with each of these three ruling for a matter of months.)

VESPASIAN (first of the Flavian Emperors) ruled 69–79 AD.

TITUS ruled 79–81 AD.

DOMITIAN (last of the Flavian dynasty) ruled 81–96 AD.

NERVA ruled 96–8 AD.

TRAJAN ruled 98–117 AD.

HADRIAN ruled 117–138 AD.

ANTONINUS PIUS ruled 138–161 AD.

MARCUS AURELIUS ruled 161–80 AD. *with* LUCIUS VERUS, who ruled 161–169 AD.

The Emperor DIOCLETIAN (286–305 AD) divided the empire into East and West, ruled by two Caesars, as centralized power became too difficult.

CONSTANTINE I, the Christian convert, ruled from 306 to 337 AD.

The Western Roman Empire lasted into the fifth century until the brief reign of the last Caesar, ironically called ROMULUS AUGUSTULUS (465–511 AD). 'Little Romulus Augustus' was a pale imitation of Romulus, the first king, and Augustus, the first Emperor of Rome.

CONSTANTINE XI, who ruled 1449–53 AD, was the last Byzantine Emperor and the last Roman Emperor, toppled by Mehmet II in 1453 when he took Constantinople.

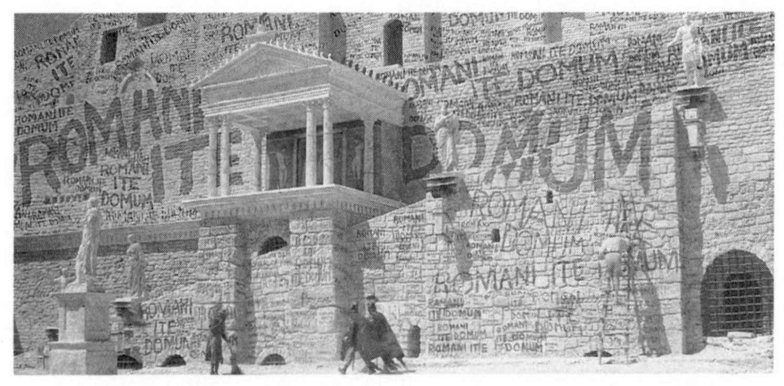

The Monty Python Guide to Latin Graffiti: **Romani, ite domum – 'Romans, go home'.**

I

Writing on the Wall – Latin Graffiti, from Pompeii's Brothel to Herculaneum's Tavernas

At the recently excavated *thermopolium*, or snack bar, in Pompeii, there's a wonderfully rude graffito:

> **NICIA CINAEDE CACATOR**
>
> **Nicias** [probably a freedman from Greece]**, you catamite shitter!**

Graphic mosaics have just been found at the Roman site of Antiochia ad Cragum in Turkey; they're meticulously designed – and extremely rude. Narcissus and Ganymede are depicted admiring what you might call their own bulging naked assets. These mosaics were used to decorate a Roman latrine, showing how the Romans beautified even the most humdrum of rooms; and how open they were about sex.

It's hard for us prudish twenty-first-century Westerners to understand this, because we're so programmed to think of the past as being innately more conservative. That principle applies particularly to Latin, the supposedly grand language.

If you want to know how everyday Romans – not Virgil, Tacitus or Julius Caesar – actually talked, then look at Roman graffiti. It still survives in great quantities, scrawled above the bar in Pompeii tavernas, scribbled on the walls of houses in Rome. The graffiti is often in very good condition, although it can be quite hard to make out – with no divisions between the words, and the letters written in a recognizable, but hard to decipher, ancient font. Once you do work it out, you'll find that, just like schoolboys today, the Romans loved their graffiti to be rude.

In the house of Claudius Eulogus in Via Dell'Abbondanza, one of Pompeii's main streets, there is a piece of graffiti with a very modern sensibility:

Move te, fellator.

Push off, cocksucker.

In the basilica in Pompeii, there's the line,

Lucilla ex corpore lucrum faciebat.

Lucilla made money from her body.

On a nearby wall, someone has written,

Sum tua aeris assibus II.

I'm yours for two bronze coins.

It wasn't just rude words they loved to write. In the Domus Tiberiana in Rome, there's a picture of a crudely drawn man with an oversized penis for a nose. Graffiti artists were also fond of drawing dogs, donkeys and horses. But they liked phalluses most.

Still, the romantic old Romans did rise above pornography in the eternal search for romantic love. Plenty of lovelorn graffiti survives, including this in the house of Pinarius Cerialis in Pompeii:

Marcellus Praenestinam amat et non curatur.

Marcellus loves Praenestina but she doesn't care for him.

Some of the writing is less graffiti – more advertisement. In Herculaneum, in a taverna's kitchen, the proprietor wrote,

XI Kalendas panem factum.

Bread is made on the eleventh of the month.

Just like in modern Italy, political graffiti was popular. In Via Nolana, Pompeii, you can see the slogan,

C. Iulium Polybium aedilem oro vos faciatis. Panem bonum fert.

I beg you to make C. Julius Polybius *aedile* [a magistrate]**. He makes good bread.**

Lovers of Roman civilization will be relieved to discover the graffiti can be high-minded, too. Some graffiti-writers cleverly referenced the great Roman authors, as Fabius Ululitremulus did in his Pompeii laundry:

Fullones ululamque cano, non arma virumque.

I sing of launderers and howling, not arms and a man.

Fabius was quoting what were then, as now, the most famous words in Roman poetry, the opening line of Virgil's *Aeneid*:

Arma virumque cano.

I sing of arms and a man.

That man was Aeneas, the Trojan survivor of the Trojan War who went on to found Rome.

Over 2,000 years later, in *Sword of Bone*, the 1942 novel about the war by Anthony Rhodes, a British officer, Stimpson, also plays on the line with his anti-military parody,

Arma meretricesque cano.

I sing of arms and prostitutes.

'Of course,' Stimpson said scornfully about his Latin lines, 'the people it's intended for won't be able to understand it, although it does sum them up so aptly.'

These clever little twists on famous lines from Latin literature were popular graffiti subjects. In Balbus's house in Pompeii, there's the simple line,

Militat omnes.

Everyone fights.

That's a play on Ovid's line in his *Amores*,

Militat omnis amans.

Every lover is a soldier.

Amores, 1.9.1

People who struggled with their gerundives and subjunctives at school will be pleased that the Romans also found their language difficult. The graffiti writer in Balbus's house should have said '*omnis*' in the singular, not '*omnes*' in the plural.

It brings to mind the wonderful scene in *Life of Brian*, where John Cleese's centurion tells off Graham Chapman's Brian for getting his Latin graffiti wrong. Chapman writes 'Romans, go home' as '*Romani eunt domus*.' John Cleese's centurion corrects it to '*Romani, ite domum*':

> Centurion: 'Romans, go home!' is an order, so you must use the . . . ?
>
> Brian: The . . . imperative.
>
> Centurion: Which is?
>
> Brian: Um, oh, oh, 'I', 'I'!
>
> Centurion: How many Romans?
>
> Brian: Plural, plural! *Ite*.

The scene was echoed in 2017, when a graffiti artist in Cambridge scrawled '*Locus in domos*' and '*Loci populum*' on a luxury housing development. The Latin doesn't mean anything. Clearly, he had put 'Local homes for local people' into Google Translate, and ended up with this gobbledegook.

In 2000, the boys of Westminster School echoed the scene again. On the school library roof they wrote, in huge letters, 'TJP ITO DOMUM'. TJP was the nickname of the then headmaster, Tristram Jones-Parry.

The boys were accused of extreme rudeness, imitating Monty Python by saying, in Latin, 'TJP, go home.' In fact, the clever little things pointed out, they weren't using the second person imperative, '*Ite domum*', meaning, 'go home'. Instead they were using the third person, singular, future active imperative, meaning, 'Let him go home.' In other words, they were politely saying that they thought their venerable headmaster was so distinguished and had done such sterling work that he deserved a graceful, glorious retirement. Too clever by half?

Some of the mistakes in Roman graffiti are comfortingly basic. One graffiti artist in Pompeii confuses his accusatives with his nominatives, writing 'pupa mea' (**my little girl**), when he should have said '**pupam meam**'. In Sallust's house in Pompeii, someone really mangles his Latin, turning **quae bella es (you who are beautiful)** into 'que bela is'. Bottom of the class, Sallust!

But let's not quibble over schoolboy mistakes – or what is often local dialect (Naples, the nearest city to Pompeii, still has its own dialect today). Let's rejoice in the moving poetry of the best graffiti, like these lines found in the Pompeii house of Caecilius Secundus:

Quisquis amat valeat, pereat qui nescit amare, bis tanto pereat, quisquis amare vetat.

Let whoever loves prosper; but let the person who doesn't know how to love die. And let the one who outlaws love die twice.

Or what about these lovely words, scrawled onto the wall of a bar in Pompeii?

Nihil durare potest tempore perpetuo;
Cum bene sol nituit, redditur oceano,
Decrescit Phoebe, quae modo fuit,
Ventorum feritas saepe fit aura levis.

Nothing can last for ever;
Once the sun has shone, it returns beneath the sea.

The Moon, once full, eventually wanes,
The violence of the winds often turns into a light breeze.

Not the sort of thing you find daubed in marker pen over the bogs in the Dog and Duck.

But even when Roman graffiti does sink into the gutter, it has the same stirring effect as the high-flown poetry – the hand that wrote it on a wall 2,000 years ago reaches out across the centuries and touches your heart.

Roman Britannia.

2

Ruling Britannia – Roman Britain, from Londinium's First Bankers to Freezing Legionaries on Hadrian's Wall

Nemo bonus Britto est.

No good man is a Briton.

Decius Magnus Eosins (309–92 AD)

There are few greater thrills in the ancient world than original inscriptions and letters in Latin. Some of the best were found as recently as 2017, during the dig for the financial news company Bloomberg's new European headquarters of the City of London, where a **Mithraeum**, a Roman **temple sacred to the god Mithras**, was found in 1954.

The temple was first unearthed under a pub in the City during work near Bank Tube station, in dramatic circumstances. In the Blitz, between September 1940 and May 1941, Nazi bombs destroyed or damaged a third of the buildings in the City. One vicious raid, on the night of 10 May 1941, obliterated practically all the buildings on the Bloomberg site.

In 1954, an 11-year-old boy, Michael Keulemans, was biking around the bombsite with his schoolmates Bob and David.

'On one of our sorties, I spotted something quite different,' Keulemans says today. 'Among all the stubs of red brick, there was a curved piece of ragstone walling interspersed with a row of red bonding tiles halfway up. I knew immediately what it was.' Keulemans rushed off to the Guildhall Museum and reported his find to Norman Cook, the curator. The curved wall he had stumbled upon was part of the apse of a Roman temple.

A team of archaeologists investigated the bombsite, just before a new office building, Bucklersbury House, was constructed. They followed the line of the curved wall and found the nearly complete floor plan of a large, rectangular Roman building. Still, they didn't know what it was, until, on the last day before construction of the office block, 18 September 1954, a workman found a Roman head. Archaeologists recognized it as the Persian god Mithras, from his characteristic Persian cap and his upwards gaze, staring at the sun.

The press went to town, including the *Daily Mail*, which splashed on its front cover with the story of 35,000 people queueing round the block to see the temple. Even Winston Churchill, then Prime Minister, intervened, to demand an extension to the excavation, during which time more staggering Roman sculptures and artefacts were found. The temple was saved and laboriously transplanted, brick by brick, to the street outside, where it was reconstructed in 1962. That reconstruction wasn't ideal – it even introduced crazy paving to the structure.

But then, in 2017, the temple was returned underground, only a few feet from its original site. During construction of the new Bloomberg HQ, archaeologists found the foundations of the original Roman temple, 23 feet below modern ground level. They have placed the temple a slight distance from its original site, to conserve those foundations.

In 2017, during this later dig to build the Bloomberg headquarters, 14,000 Roman artefacts were found in a miraculous state of preservation. That's because the

Mithraeum was on the banks of the River Walbrook, a small river feeding into the Thames. The wet mud prevented air getting to the wood, stopping it from rotting.

It preserved an extraordinary array of Roman finds: the bones of sacrificed chickens; tiny Roman leather shoes, worn by a child; combs; brooches; pewter plates; spearheads; and a lead plaque of a leaping bull, thought to be the zodiac symbol Taurus. The finds also included 300 brooches and dozens of different shoes, from a soldier's hob-nailed boot to a lacy, perforated **carbatina** – the Christian Louboutin **shoe** of its day. A bread oven was discovered, as were the remains of north African cockroaches which fed off piles of grain.

There's a charming, tiny, amber amulet, perhaps worn by a child, in the shape of a gladiator's helmet. Valuable amber was thought to have magical protective properties by the Romans, and the helmet shape was symbolic of protection.

Most important of all, though, are wooden tablets, with some of the earliest Roman inscriptions in Britain. Romans wrote letters by scoring their words into wax, set into wooden tablets, with an iron stylus – or a sharp piece of pencil-shaped metal. 200 of these styli were discovered during the Bloomberg dig.

Early Londoners wrote letters in soot-blackened beeswax with that stylus. Once the recipient had read the letter, he smoothed the surface with a heated spatula and wrote another letter in the wax – like a primitive Etch A Sketch. The writer often carved so deeply into the wax that he accidentally left his words etched into the wood beneath. So, although the wax has long since rotted away, inscriptions can still be read in the wood.

Buried under 20ft of mud for nearly 2,000 years, these simple Roman wooden tablets are the earliest handwritten documents ever found in Britain.

Among the 405 unearthed by archaeologists, they include the first known reference to London – and the first IOU. Most of the documents, written in that wax on a folding wooden frame, date from between 55 and 85 AD. Among the tablets are financial records, legal documents, and instructions for servants running errands.

Historians believe one tablet refers to a Roman proverb – **per panem et salem – by bread and salt –** requesting repayment of a debt:

Rogo te per panem et salem ut quam primum mittas denarios viginti sex in victoriatis et denarios decem Paterionis.

I ask you by bread and salt that you send the 26 denarii in *victoriati* and the 10 denarii of Paterio as soon as possible.

The tablets, made from wood recycled from wine casks imported from the Continent, give a remarkable picture of a Roman London teeming with businessmen, lawyers, tradesmen and slaves. Within a few years of being established, the city was already a whirring mix of commerce, eating, socializing and fashion.

The letters also provide an insight into the Roman postal system. The writer carved the address into the outer, wooden surface of the folding boxes, tied it up and sent his slave to deliver it. Addresses were simpler then, with no house numbers – just the names of neighbours. One address reads:

Dabes Iunio cupario contra Catullus.

You will give this to Junius the cooper, opposite Catullus's house.

The oldest tablet which can be dated exactly is a letter between two London businessmen, acknowledging a debt – then, as now, the city revolved around money. References to a consul of the time mean it can be dated to 57 AD – only a few years after Londinium was founded by the Emperor Claudius in 43 AD. The letter, dated the sixth day before the Ides of January – or 8 January – reads,

Tibullus Venusti libertus scripsi et dico me debere Grato Spuri liberto denarios cu ex s pretio.

I, Tibullus, the freedman of Venustus, have written and say that I owe Gratus, the freedman of Spurius, 105 denarii.

Another tablet contains the address,

Londinio Mogontio.

In London, to Mogontius.

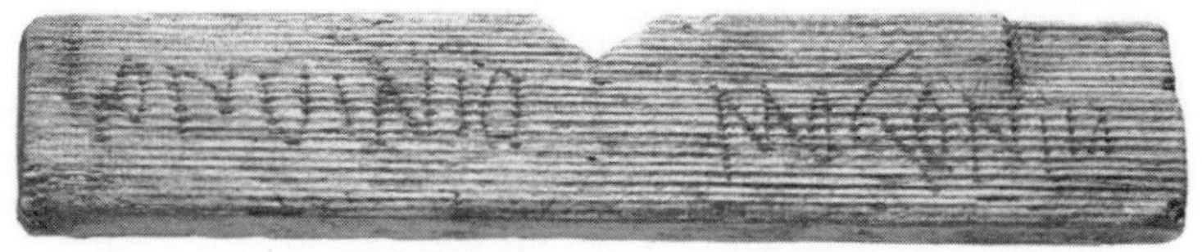

Londinio Mogontio – "In London, to Mogontius". The earliest surviving mention of London, c. 65–80 AD.

This, staggeringly, is the earliest surviving reference to London *anywhere*. From where it was found in the layers of mud, archaeologists have dated it to 65–80 AD.

One letter, the earliest readable tablet, which dates back to 43 AD, in the first year of Roman rule under Emperor Claudius, shows Roman London was a busy shopping centre full of loan sharks. Written to a sloppy businessman, it says:

> **Quia per forum totum gloriantur se te faenerasse.**
>
> **They are boasting through the whole market that you have lent them money.**

Other finds include a soldier's will from 67 AD, discovered in the foundations of Britain's earliest law firm. There are writing exercises, too, perhaps from the first London school, listing the letters of the alphabet – ABCD – and a series of Roman numerals. Another tablet records a debt to Crispus, a brewer, for supplying nearly 3,000 pints of beer.

Many of the wooden documents relate to records of financial transactions. One 62 AD tablet is a Roman receipt for 20 truckloads of provision from Verulamium (now St Albans), just a year after Boadicea's forces devastated swathes of Roman Britain.

129 people are mentioned in the letters, including Roman emperors and aristocrats, slaves and a soldier who had fought for Emperor Augustus. No women are mentioned, but London was already an international city. There are references to Roman and Celtic names, as well as soldiers from Gaul and the Rhineland – modern France and Germany.

1,800 years ago, that Temple of Mithras would have been crammed with dozens of sweaty Roman legionaries, slaves and merchants, worshipping the ancient Persian god.

New worshippers – male only – stood naked in the middle of the temple. As part of the blood-curdling ritual, they were given the impression they were about to be killed. A naked new member would kneel down, while a long-term member stood above him, his sword raised, as if to slice his neck off.

Other new members would be threatened by archers, all set to launch arrows at them. There was probably heavy drinking.

The building was later converted, it's thought, into a temple to Bacchus, the Roman god of wine, before it was abandoned in the late fourth century. Even when it was built, the windowless temple was underground, lit by torches and lamps, artfully placed behind statues of the god, with the illumination reflected in a square well.

Burning incense wafted through the temple, filling it with smoke. The **pater** – **father** – of the religion (a kind of priest) would pray out loud to the god, crying, **'Nama'**, a Persian greeting word, meaning something like **'Hail'**. The pater's cries overlapped with the frantic squawks of chickens sacrificed in Mithras's name, their blood gushing over the temple altar.

And over it all stood a huge statue of Mithras himself, staring up at the sun, surrounded by signs of the zodiac, as he slaughtered an effigy of a bull. The bull-slaughter – or 'tauroctony' – was thought to signify creation, transformation, the human place in the universe, and worship of the sun and the moon.

The Mithraeum, built of Kentish ragstone and brick in around 240 AD, was right at the heart of Roman London. It was close to the Roman **forum** (**marketplace**) – the heart of the Roman government of Londinium. The forum was home to the first offices in London, too. The word 'office' grew out of the Latin, **officium**, which originally meant **a helpful service**, duty or task – all of which a good office still provides. *Officium* then came to mean a place of work where those duties were performed.

Early Roman offices were often in basilicas, from *basilike*, the Greek for 'royal'. Basilicas were courts of justice for Roman emperors, with adjoining offices, before early Christian churches, built on the same ground plan, acquired the name 'basilica'. Londinium's basilica, built in 70 AD and expanded in around 100 AD, was enormous: five acres and three storeys high, forming one side of a huge forum. At its height, it was the biggest basilica north of the Alps, housing law courts, a treasury, shrine, assembly hall and those offices for city government.

By the early third century AD, Londinium's wall enclosed 330 acres, making it the biggest town in Roman Britain and smaller than only four towns in Gaul. You can still see substantial remains of the red Kentish sandstone and ragstone walls on foundations of puddled clay, flints and ragstone, with hard, white, lime mortar. Outside the wall, there was a defensive **fossa** (**ditch**). Inside the wall, there was the **vallum** (**bank**), which gives us our word 'wall'.

The basilica was largely destroyed in the late third century AD – that was possibly as a punishment for Londinium supporting the rogue general Carausius (died 293 AD), who declared himself emperor over an area of Britannia and northern Gaul he called **Imperium Britanniarum** – the **Empire of the Britains**. Still, fragments of the basilica survive beneath Leadenhall Market. If you ask very nicely, they'll let you see the best surviving stone foundations in the basement of a barber's shop on the corner of Leadenhall Market and Gracechurch Street.

Londinium's Roman amphitheatre, where gladiators fought to the death, is only a few hundred yards away from the Mithraeum, too, beneath London's Guildhall. London's Roman amphitheatre was excavated in 1987 beneath the Guildhall Art Gallery. Among the discoveries was a timber sliding trapdoor – used, it's thought, to release wild animals into the arena.

London's Temple of Mithras is shaped very like early Christian churches – which were, in fact, inspired by Roman temples like this – with a rectangular plan and a semi-circular altar at one end. There's a central nave or passageway, which would have had a mosaic pavement, divided into seven areas, each decorated with its own symbols and gods. Those symbols and gods would have appealed to different Roman professions.

There would have been an image of an oil lamp and a tiara, symbols of Venus, the goddess of love – new bridegrooms in the temple would have bellowed a heartfelt 'Nama' to Venus. A picture of a lance and helmet, symbolizing Mars, the god of war, was favoured by legionaries, who were particularly fond of Mithras, and exported his cult across the Roman Empire.

And then, at the far end of the temple, right by the altar, there was a picture of a Persian cap, signifying the great god Mithras himself. This spot would probably have been reserved for the pater. Right behind him, raised on steps, was the statue of Mithras, slaughtering a bull. It's this statue's head that was, miraculously, found in 1954.

Below the statue, there was a stone screen – which also, amazingly, survives. Here Mithras slaughters a bull in a cave, while a dog, scorpion and snake feast off the dying creature. Around him are depicted the 12 signs of the zodiac. Several cow skulls have been found in a nearby well, probably left as ritual gifts to Mithras.

On the screen, on one side of Mithras, a torch-bearer holds a torch aloft; on the other side, another one holds his torch down, extinguishing it. Mithras was often equated with Sol, the sun god: the two torch-bearers show the power of light and dark, standing for life and death. Four small holes, found behind the statue plinth, are thought to have carried torches, too, to create spooky light effects. To the left of the altar, a timber tank held water, used in water-sprinkling rituals and to reflect the light.

The stone screen gives us a clue as to who built the temple. A Latin inscription on it reads,

> **Ulpius Silvanus miles factus Arausione emeritus legionis II Augustae votum solvit.**

Ulpius Silvanus, veteran of the second Augustan legion, fulfilled his vow: he was initiated at Orange.

That refers to Orange in Provence, France, a crucial city in Roman Gaul. In other words, this spectacular temple might have been paid for by a French veteran of a legion founded by Augustus, the first Roman Emperor.

How fitting that the earliest Roman financial document in Britain should be found on the site of the new Bloomberg building, the billion-pound office of the future.

It's got it all: a state-of-the-art TV studio, two cinema-lecture halls, an art gallery, a wellness centre and a mothers' room, all crammed full of millions of pounds' worth of contemporary art. It's one of the greenest office buildings in the world, with rainwater feeding off the roof to cool the lightbulbs inside and flush the loos.

The Bloomberg building has even reconstructed an ancient Roman road, Watling Street, which runs in a tunnel right through the middle of the office block. Under the Romans, Watling Street originally ran through London, across the Thames, from **Dubris** (**Dover**) to **Viroconium** (**Wroxeter, Shropshire**).

But the Bloomberg Building's real claim to fame is unique – it has Londinium's greatest Roman temple in the basement.

We know about the kind of thing those Roman soldiers in Britain would have eaten, thanks to letters sent home by legionaries from near Hadrian's Wall.

They benefited from the supply lines through the Empire, along those famous, straight Roman roads, which brought rich food from the Mediterranean. And so the legionaries demand all sorts of luxury items: Massic wine (a fine Italian vintage), fish, semolina, lentils, garlic, olives and olive oil. They turn their noses up at the local Pictish fare: pork fat, cereal, spices, roe deer and venison. There are many mentions, too, of **cervesa** and **callum** – that is, **beer** and **pork scratchings**, and all 1,000 years before the great British pub had been invented.

The demand for fine food hit a peak at the festival of the Roman goddess of chance, Fors Fortuna, when the people had a hog roast, washed down with great quantities of wine. They claimed the wine was **ad sacrum divae**: **for religious use** – an early version of the old 'I only drink for medicinal purposes' ploy.

In the frozen wastes of the north, legionaries even asked their relations back home in Gaul for good, thick, woollen pants. A surviving letter from Gaul to a freezing legionary in Vindolanda, Northumberland, lists the contents of the care package he's getting: **Paria udonum ab Sattua solearum duo et subligariorum duo** (**socks, two pairs of sandals and two pairs of underpants**).

The Vindolanda tablets, including the underpants letter, were discovered by Robin Birley (1935–2008) and his father Eric Birley (1906–95) in 1973. They found them in a pile of Roman sewage on a windswept hill fort in the middle of the wilds of Northumberland.

Sifting through the mixture of ancient sewage, rotten bracken and straw and the contents of several decades' full of Roman rubbish bins, Robin Birley didn't think much at first when he came across a handful of half-burnt, sodden slices of oak, each about the size of a postcard.

Then, suddenly, he spotted a few faded vertical and horizontal marks in ink – Roman ink, made out of gum arabic, carbon and water. He had found it! The Holy Grail – the elusive thing experts on Roman Britain had been in search of for centuries: letters to and from the Roman soldiers who had garrisoned Britain from 43 to 410 AD. Dr Birley had stumbled upon the Geordie Dead Sea Scrolls.

The Vindolanda Tablets – 1,000 pieces of birch, alder and oak unturfed by Dr Birley over the next decade – give an unparalleled, moving and often very funny insight into the life of the Roman soldier stuck miles away from home at the end of the first century AD. The letters tend to be from officers, inevitably more literate than legionaries.

The tablets were found in the ruins of the **praetorium**, the **residence of the officers** commanding the Vindolanda units from 90 to 120 AD, just before Hadrian's Wall was built from 122 to 130 AD. The wall was eventually to stretch 74 miles from Solway Firth in the west to Wallsend on the River Tyne in the east, just south of today's border with Scotland.

How the soldiers miss their beloved family and friends back in Gaul – that's where most of them came from. How they long for delicious, fine Italian wine. How they dread the attacks of the vicious Picts – the woad-encrusted savages from the north whose raids were to be held off by the new wall of turf and stone stretching across the neck of England. But most of all, how cold they are up here in the frozen north, a few miles from modern Hexham.

The Vindolanda tablets look like little wooden postcards, often painstakingly knitted back together from fragments, relating in the cramped hands of more than 280 correspondents what life was really like in the Roman Empire. Contrary to popular belief, Romans didn't do all their writing by carving into stone – or in wooden frames with wax panels, like the letters found at the Mithraeum temple in London. Most Roman letters were written on papyrus – the paper made from the papyrus plant grown in the blistering heat of the Egyptian Nile.

There's not much call for papyrus plants in Northumberland, and the wax and wood technique required far too much raw material. So the Vindolanda officers settled for these simple leaves of wood, 1 to 3 millimetres thick, scratched with a reed pen dipped into an inkwell. The wood was all local.

Once written on, these slim wooden letters were often folded, leaving an imprint of wet ink on the opposite page that can still be seen. Just as with a postcard today, Romans then wrote the addressee on the right-hand side of the card, with the name of the sender below preceded by **a** or **ab** – meaning **from**. Much of the letter was written by a professional scribe, with the sender closing the letter in his own hand, writing **Vale frater – Goodbye, brother**.

Among these delicate little fragments, there are military documents reporting the strength and activities of the Vindolanda garrison. Also revealed are details of the domestic administration of this remote outpost. Along with those all-important pants, the Romans are desperate for **subuclae** (**vests**), **abollae** (**thick, heavy cloaks**) and **cubitoria** – a full **dinner service**.

But what really gets the heart racing are the real day-to-day lives of the soldiers, their family and friends. Here is brother writing to brother – 'Vittius Adiutor eagle-bearer of the Second Augustan Legion to Cassius Saecularis, his little brother, very many greetings'.

Most moving of all is a letter from Claudia Severa to her sister, Sulpicia Lepidina, the wife of a big cheese at Vindolanda, Flavius Cerialis, prefect of the Ninth Cohort of Batavians. 'Oh, how I want you to come to my birthday party – you'll make the day so much more enjoyable. I so hope you can make it. Goodbye, sister, my dearest soul.'

'Anima mea desideratissima' – **'My most longed-for soul'** – Claudia calls Sulpicia in another letter. You can almost hear the wrenching apart of the hearts, divided by the greatest imperial project in the history of the world.

What a wrench it is for us, too, almost 2,000 years on, to read how those hearts were brought together by these rotten, scorched, little slips of oak, inscribed with words that sound as fresh as if they were written this morning.

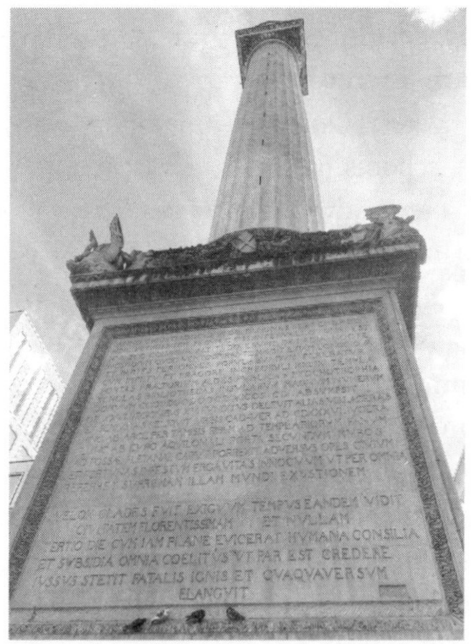

The Monument's Latin inscription: the pigeons are sitting where the anti-Catholic Latin was erased.

LONDON'S BEST LATIN QUOTATION

Latin continued – and continues – as a lingua franca, a common language, on more recent British monuments, including the Monument, the one to the Great Fire built by Christopher Wren and Robert Hooke in 1677. The Latin text is still there today. Below is the English translation, with the most dramatic phrases from the Latin in brackets:

> **In the year of Christ** (**anno Christi**) 1666, the second day of September, eastward from hence, at the distance of 202 feet (**the height of this column – huiusce columnae altitudo**), about **midnight** (**media nocte**), a most terrible **fire** (**incendium**) broke out, which, driven on by a high wind, not only wasted the adjacent parts, but also places very remote,

with incredible noise and fury (**cum impetu et fragore incredibili**): it consumed 89 churches, the city gates, Guildhall, many public structures, hospitals, schools, libraries, a vast number of stately edifices, 13,200 dwelling-houses, 400 streets; of 26 wards, it utterly destroyed 15, and left eight others shattered and half burnt. The **ruins of the city** (**urbis cadaver**) were 436 acres, **from the Tower by the Thames side to the Temple church** (**ab Arce per Tamesis ripam at Templariorum fanum**), and from the north-east gate along the city wall to Holborn-bridge. To the **estates and fortunes of the citizens** (**opes civium et fortunas**) it was merciless, but to their lives very favourable, that it might in all things resemble **the last conflagration of the world** (**supremam mundi exhaustionem**).

The destruction was sudden; for in a small space of time the same city was seen most flourishing, and reduced to nothing. Three days after, when this **fatal fire** (**fatalis ignis**) had baffled all human counsels and endeavours in the opinion of all, as it were by the will of Heaven it stopped, and on every side was **extinguished** (**elanguit**).

Look at the bottom of the Monument inscription and you'll see there's a rough area where a line has been rubbed out. That line originally read: **Sed Furor Papisticus Qui Tamdiu Patravit Nondum Restingvitur** (**But Popish frenzy, which wrought such horrors, is not yet quenched**). It was added in 1681, when anti-Catholic sentiment was raging. The line wasn't chiselled out until 1830, after Catholic Emancipation in 1829.

A fresco in the Lupanar, Pompeii's brothel. Look out for the woman's early bra.

3

Sex in Rome and the Rudest Poem in Latin

Before we wax lyrical about the very real, sublime beauties of Latin love poetry, here's a trigger warning. They did things very differently – and very rudely – in Rome.

As the late classics don James Noel Adams (1943–2021) put it in *The Latin Sexual Vocabulary* (1982), Roman society was rich in obscenity, like ours – though their obscenity sometimes seems exotic to us. The Romans shouted swear words into thin air to ward off evil spirits. When celebrating military victories, triumphant generals wore phallic amulets around their necks. In the town of Lavinium, the townspeople cursed for a whole month to salute Liber, the god of wine.

Even the holiest of men admitted to his urges:

Da mihi castitatem et continentiam – sed noli modo.

Give me chastity and continency – but not yet.

St Augustine of Hippo (354–430 AD), *Confessions*, 8.7

And now those of a nervous disposition, please look away. And those of a sex-obsessed disposition, prepare yourself for the most disgusting poem ever written in Latin. It's *Carmen 16* by Catullus:

THE RUDEST POEM IN LATIN

Pedicabo ego vos et irrumabo,
Aureli pathice et cinaede Furi,
qui me ex versiculis meis putastis,
quod sunt molliculi, parum pudicum.
Nam castum esse decet pium poetam
ipsum, versiculos nihil necesse est;
qui tum denique habent salem ac leporem,
si sunt molliculi ac parum pudici,
et quod pruriat incitare possunt,
non dico pueris, sed his pilosis
qui duros nequeunt movere lumbos.
Vos, quod milia multa basiorum
legistis, male me marem putatis?
Pedicabo ego vos et irrumabo.

I will sodomize you and face-fuck you,
cocksucker Aurelius and bottom bitch Furius,
who think, from my little verses,
because they're a little soft, that I have no shame.
For it is right for the devoted poet to be chaste himself,
but it isn't necessary that his verses should be.
Verses which then indeed have taste and charm,
If they are a little soft and have no shame,

And because they can incite an itch,
And I don't mean in boys, but in
Those hairy men who can't move their loins.
You, because you've read about my many thousands of kisses,
you think me less of a man?
I will sodomize you and face-fuck you.

I'm afraid Ovid wasn't much cleaner. He wouldn't have lasted a second these days, with his principal, evil dating tip – rape. Here he is in his *Ars Amatoria* (The Art of Loving):

Grata est vis ista puellis;
Quod iuvat, invitae saepe dedisse volunt.
Quaecumque est Veneris subita violata rapina,
Gaudet, et inprobitas muneris instar habet.
At quae cum posset cogi, non tacta recessit,
Ut simulet vultu gaudia, tristis erit.
Vim passa est Phoebe, vis est allata sorori;
Et gratus raptae raptor uterque fuit.

It's force that pleases girls: what delights
is to have given them what they wanted often, against their will.
Whoever is taken in love's sudden violation
is pleased, and finds wickedness is a tribute.
And the girl who might have been forced, and escapes intact,

will be sad, even if she simulates delight in her expression.
Phoebe was taken by force, force was offered to her sister:
and both rape victims were grateful to those who raped them.

In *Ars Amatoria*, Ovid also had the wicked view that a drunk girl is an available girl:

Turpe iacens mulier multo madefacta Lyaeo:
digna est concubitus quoslibet illa pati.

A woman lying down, completely drunk after lots of wine, is an ugly sight. She's fair game for anyone to have his way with.

Ovid was rudely blunt about the effect of ancient beer goggles: 'Plain though you are, you'll look a goddess to drunken eyes.'

Romans were keen on the double entendre, too. In Plautus's second-century BC comedy *The Ghost*, a young, drunk man leans towards a young woman and addresses her cleavage.

Tun me ais ma-m-ma-madere?

Are you saying I'm ti-t-ti-tipsy?

The stuttered word **ma-m-ma-madere** is a play on **mamma**, Latin for **breast**, as in mammary. It was also a Latin word for mother. By the way, if you think Plautus is a bit lowbrow, there's always Terence, responsible for *the* great statement on humankind:

Homo sum, nil humani alienum a me puto.

I am a man, and I think nothing human is alien to me.

In *On the Nature of Things*, the poet Lucretius (*c.* 99–55 BC) explains why prostitutes aren't just trying to give men more pleasure when they exaggerate their erotic movements during sex.

Idque sua causa consuerunt scorta moveri,
ne complerentur crebro gravidaeque iacerent.

And so prostitutes have their own reason for their wriggling movements, to stop themselves from conceiving too often and being laid up through pregnancy.

These erotic exercises, Lucretius says, are more fun for men, but they are 'obviously something our wives have no use for', implying their function was simply to produce children. This may help to explain the large number of brothels in Roman towns and cities.

Where there is love, there are also erotic dreams, I'm afraid. Horace is one of the first writers to describe a wet dream:

Tum immundo somnia visu nocturnam vestem maculant ventremque supinum.

As I lay on my back, dreams then turned to obscene fantasies that stained my nightclothes and stomach.

Satires, 1.5.84–5

That word for stain, *maculant*, is where we get the word 'immaculate' – or 'unstained' – from.

Intriguingly, homosexuality wasn't recognized in Rome. If a man had sexual relations with another man, it was a demonstration of power and superiority, not any particular sexual leaning. It was something you did to slaves and the young – your subordinates.

Where there is sex, there is impotence. Petronius (*c.* 27–66 AD), in his novel *Satyricon* (turned into a film in 1969 by Federico Fellini), described the impotence of his anti-hero, Encolpius, a student on the run for murder. Petronius cleverly played on original passages from Virgil's *Aeneid*, which described Dido giving the cold shoulder to her old lover Aeneas – and a young warrior, Euryalus, who droops as he dies. The joke is that Encolpius is haranguing his ineffectual, drooping penis:

Illa solo fixos oculos aversa tenebat, nec magis incepto vultum sermone movetur quam lentae salices lassove papavera collo.

It turned away with its eyes fixed on the ground, and no more changed its expression at the speech I'd begun than pliant willows or poppies on their tired necks.

Petronius wondered why men and women indulge in sex at all, other than to procreate:

Foeda est in coitu et brevis voluptas
et taedet Veneris statim peractae.

The pleasure in sex is disgusting and short, and is immediately wearisome once the act of love is over.

Petronius was in the minority among Roman poets – they were usually devoted to sex. Ovid described how his mistress Corinna came to him one sultry afternoon and bared all before his eyes, 'not a blemish to be seen', inviting him to make love to her:

Quos umeros, quales vidi tetigique lacertos! Forma papillarum quam fuit apta premi!

What shoulders; what arms did I see and touch! What shapely breasts, so right for me to press!

After rhapsodizing over her attributes, the poet continues:

Nudam pressi corpus ad usque meum. Cetera quis nescit?

I held her naked body close to mine and . . . who doesn't know the rest?

The young Christopher Marlowe (1564–93) translated this poem at Cambridge:

Proveniant medii sic mihi saepe dies!

Jove, send me more such after-noones as this!

For Ovid, sex was the ultimate prize. In his *Amores*, he described how the soldier may win everlasting glory by dying in battle; the unscrupulous merchant may pile up wealth before meeting a watery end at sea. But the lover can think of no better way to die than during sex.

At mihi contingat Veneris languescere motu,
cum moriar, medium solvar et inter opus.

A hot death is the one I ask for, expiring in my mistress's arms, meeting my end, mid-act, in the bed of love.

Amores, 2.10.36

He ends by hoping that some mourner, shedding tears at his funeral, will look at his headstone and say, 'Well, that was a fitting end for the life you lived.'

How graphic the Romans were about their sex tips. Here is Ovid in *Ars Amatoria* on how to avoid an early climax.

Sed neque tu dominam velis maioribus usus
defice, nec cursus anteat illa tuos.

But don't let your mistress down by piling on too much sail, and make sure she doesn't reach port before your own ship.

It's much better, Ovid wrote, for a couple to reach their goal at the same time: 'That's the summit of bliss, when man and woman sink back in one another's arms, equally vanquished.' He proceeds to give some direct, unabashed sex advice.

Cum loca reppereris, quae tangi femina gaudet, non obstet, tangas quominus illa, pudor.

Once you find those parts a woman loves to be touched, don't be ashamed of touching them.

He continues with a lyrical description of the reward you will see in the lady's face: 'You will see her eyes lighting up with flickering gleams, like sunlight glittering on a clear brook.'

In *Amores*, Ovid accepted the infidelity of women and what they will do with their lovers:

Illic nec voces nec verba iuvantia cessent,
spondaque lasciva mobilitate tremat.

There they speak plenty of loving words of encouragement and make the bed shake with unrestrained movements.

But, at all costs, Ovid says, be discreet and keep it all in the bedroom. 'Put on an honest face along with your dress,' he continues, 'blush and make no confession of the naughty fun you've had . . . Cheat people, cheat me . . . but don't let me see; let me enjoy my foolish credulity.'

The devil makes works for idle adulterers' hands, says Ovid. One of the products of a slave economy for the well-to-do was plenty of **leisure** (**otium**). This meant men could make a risk-free move on wives thanks to inattentive or absent husbands.

Ovid jokingly transposed this theme back to the Trojan War. While Agamemnon was off fighting for the Greeks in the Trojan War, his cousin Aegisthus was busy seducing his wife, Clytemnestra, at home. Ovid says it wasn't hatred of Agamemnon that motivated Aegisthus (the traditional version of the story) but the sight of the beautiful Clytemnestra every day – and having nothing to do.

Quaeritis, Aegisthus quare sit factus adulter?
In promptu causa est: desidiosus erat.

You ask why Aegisthus became an adulterer? The cause was right there: he had time on his hands.

You'll see that the Latin for **adulterer** is almost exactly the same word – **adulter**.

Just as Ovid taught Romans how to become good lovers, so in his ***Remedia Amoris*** (**Cures for Love**) he told them how to get out of bad relationships. 'I'll set hearts free from love's chains,' he boasts. 'I'm the Great Liberator.'

One way to end an affair is to concentrate on a woman's least charming physical feature when you're in bed together.

Et pudet, et dicam: Venerem quoque iunge figura,
qua minime iungi quamque decere putas.

I'm embarrassed to say it but say it, I will: you should adopt a sexual position you think's least good, least attractive for the act.

Ovid ended his *Art of Love* by advising lovers not to let windows light up the whole bedroom: 'Most of your body is best left in gloom.' Now he makes the point again but in reverse, to make your lover less attractive: 'You should also have your windows let in all the daylight; that way, your eyes can take in all her parts and not be taken in.' Best, too, to see her before she's put her make-up on:

Proderit et subito, cum se non finxerit ulli, ad dominam celeres mane tulisse gradus.

You'll also find it useful to pay a sudden visit early in the morning, before she has put on her disguise for anyone's benefit.

Rem., 341

Nil desperandum! Don't despair. Not all Roman poets were so ruthlessly horrible about women. They weren't just sex mad. They also reached the higher parts of human emotion in their love poetry – as you'll see in the next chapter.

The Sappho fresco, Pompeii, c. 55–79 AD. Not in fact Sappho, but a rich woman of Pompeii, with gold earrings and gold-threaded hair, sucking on a stylus and holding her wax writing tablets.

4

True Romance – the Great Latin Love Poets

The most famous Roman love poet was Catullus (84–54 BC) – who could also be wonderfully crude, as we saw in *Carmen 16* (**Pedicabo ego vos et irrumabo – I will sodomize you and face-fuck you**).

In 25 of his poems, Catullus wrote about his beloved Lesbia, widely believed to have been the Roman aristocrat Clodia Metelli. By convention, love poets used a pseudonym for their mistresses to avoid any social embarrassment. Lesbia was said to be highly intelligent, poetic and extremely keen on the act of love – and she wasn't a lesbian.

The most famous Catullus poem to Lesbia is number five. Its most memorable lines are:

Vivamus, mea Lesbia, atque amemus rumoresque senum severiorum omnes unius aestimemus assis!

Let us live, my own Lesbia, and let us love, and, as for the gossip of grumpy old men, let's value it at one penny!

Da mi basia mille, deinde centum,
Dein mille altera, dein secunda centum. Deinde usque altera mille, deinde centum.

Give me a thousand kisses, then a hundred, then another thousand, then a second hundred, then yet another thousand, then a hundred.

Carmen 5

Catullus had fallen in love with Lesbia at first sight. His love poems to her veer from intense passion to a burning hatred. For this sophisticated woman, love was a game but, for the earnest young poet, it was all-consuming. In another poem, he calls himself **vesano – crazy for love**.

Besotted in the early days of their affair, Catullus asks Lesbia a question.

Quaeris, quot mihi basiationes
tuae, Lesbia, sint satis superque.

Lesbia, you ask how many kisses on your lips are enough – and to spare – for me.

He answers the question himself:

Tam te basia multa basiare
uesano satis et super Catullo est,
quae nec pernumerare curiosi
possint nec mala fascinare lingua.

More than enough for your crazy Catullus would be more kisses kissed than the curious could calculate or the evil-tongued know how to conjure up.

Lesbia tired of Catullus – Dorothy Parker could see why. In an imaginary letter from Lesbia to a friend, Parker warned against taking a poet as a lover:

It's just the same – a quarrel or a kiss
Is but a tune to play upon his pipe.
He's always hymning that or wailing this;
Myself, I much prefer the business type.

When Lesbia moved on to another lover, Catullus also wrote to himself about heartache:

Miser Catulle, desinas ineptire,
et quod vides perisse perditum ducas.

Catullus, you wretch, you must stop being a fool, and count as lost what you see is lost.

Catullus knew Lesbia didn't deserve his love or even his friendship because of her faithlessness, but he couldn't stop desiring her as a woman.

Odi et amo. Quare id faciam, fortasse requiris. Nescio, sed fieri sentio et excrucior.

I hate her and I love her. Perhaps you ask how I can do this. I don't know, but I feel it so, and it's sheer torture.

We get 'odious' from the word **odi** – **I hate**. It also appears in the most snobbish line in Latin:

Odi profanum vulgus et arceo.

I hate the common crowd and avoid them.

Horace, *Odes* 3.1

Mad with bitterness, Catullus asked two acquaintances to deliver this nastily pornographic message:

Cum suis vivat valeatque moechis quos simul complexa tenet trecentos, nullum amans vere, sed identidem omnium ilia rumpens.

Let her live and enjoy her lovers, embracing them all at once in their hundreds, not truly loving any of them but again and again rupturing their loins.

The ugliness of these lines is suddenly undercut by an unforgettable image that crystallizes what Catullus has lost. Lesbia, in Catullus's eyes, had all the emotional feeling of a piece of sharpened iron, while his love for her was as delicate as a flower. The blade only needed to touch the flower to destroy it.

Nec meum respectet ut ante amorem
qui illius culpa cecidit velut prati
ultimi flos praetereunte postquam
tactus aratro est.

And let her not look to my love, as once before, because, thanks to her, it has fallen like a flower at the edge of a meadow, brushed by the passing plough.

In the pain of his rejection, Catullus imagined Lesbia reduced to performing degrading sexual services for poor citizens in the back streets of Rome.

Nunc in quadriviis et angiportis glubit magnanimos Remi nepotes.

Now, at street-corners and in alleyways, she saps Remus's magnanimous descendants.

The verb he chooses here (**glubit** – **saps**) is normally used of stripping the bark from a tree. The grandiose adjective next to it, **magnanimos** (almost identical in English: **magnanimous**), emphasizes the degradation of both parties. The effect is something like 'wanks off the splendid sons of Albion'.

Catullus was less tortured when he gave dating tips to an acquaintance. He suggested that taking a bath occasionally might improve his luck. He was responding to a rumour that his friend had 'a really rank beast' dwelling in his armpits, 'a ferocious billy-goat' that is 'an affront to the nostrils'. What pretty girl would go to bed with such a creature?

Noli admirari quare tibi femina nulla, Rufe, velit tenerum supposuisse femur,

Don't be surprised, Rufus, that no woman is willing to place her soft thighs under yours.

Note the Latin for **thigh** – **femur**, as in the English word for the thigh bone.

The poet Tibullus (55–19 BC), writing under Emperor Augustus, was just as jealous as Catullus – in his case, about his mistress, Delia:

Iam Delia furtim nescio quem tacita callida nocte fovet.

Now, stealthily, my cunning Delia is keeping some unknown man warm in the silence of the night.

Tibullus worries that Delia is being unfaithful to him. She swears she isn't but, he says, it's hard to take her at her word; doesn't she keep denying his own existence to her husband? It's the classic lover's dilemma: if his mistress can be unfaithful to her husband, why not to him as well? As the late financier Sir Jimmy Goldsmith put it, 'If you marry your mistress, you create a vacancy.'

Tibullus's contemporary, Propertius (50–15 BC), was less jealous than mad with longing. Catullus had Lesbia. Propertius had Cynthia, revered in these famous lines.

Cynthia prima fuit; Cynthia finis erit.

Cynthia was the first; Cynthia will be the last.

He tells his mistress she is everything he holds precious in his life: that's why he wants her to end her stay in Baiae and return to Rome.

Tu mihi sola domus, tu, Cynthia, sola parentes, omni tu nostrae tempore deliciae.

You alone, Cynthia, are my home, you alone my parents, you at all times my heart's delight.

Baiae, now a splendid ruin on the Bay of Naples, was a favourite haunt of the idle rich on the coast of Campania, where the Roman jet set went to have fun in summer. Propertius concludes his poem with a heartfelt plea:

Multis ista dabunt litora discidium,

litora quae fuerunt castis inimica puellis: ah pereant Baiae, crimen amoris, aquae!

Those shores will break many love pacts: shores dangerous to girls who would be faithful. Damn you, waters of Baiae, you crime against love!

Propertius ends on a sad note. Cynthia has proved false, her head turned by being the subject of his verse. Just as his poetry once elevated her, so now it will bring her down, deservedly:

Falsa est ista tuae, mulier, fiducia formae, olim elegis nimium facta superba meis.

It has deceived you, my lady, your confidence in your beauty – you who were once made far too proud by my poems.

He asks for wrinkles to disfigure her once lovely face and regret for past arrogance to mar her declining years: 'Learn to fear the outcome of your lovely looks.'

The exhaustion of love is so great that Horace begins his fourth book of Odes by complaining to the goddess of love that he is now too old to write love poetry.

Intermissa, Venus, diu rursus bella moves? Parce, precor, precor.

Are you stirring up war again, Venus, when it has been abandoned for so long? Spare me, I beg you, I beg you!

Love was at once the most agonizing and the funniest subject in Rome. Horace warns Maecenas, his friend and patron, not to try the trick of giving him garlic at dinner.

At si quid umquam tale concupiveris, iocose Maecenas, precor manum puella savio opponat tuo, extrema et in sponda cubet.

But if ever you fancy playing such a trick, Maecenas, you joker, I hope your girl stops your kiss with her hand and lies as far away from you in bed as she can.

For all his attempts to give up romance, Horace finds himself under orders from 'cruel' Venus once more. He admits to being in love again, this time with the beautiful Glycera.

Urit me Glycerae nitor splendentis Pario marmore purius: urit grata protervitas et vultus nimium lubricus aspici.

Glycera's beauty burns me with its sheen more flawless than Parian marble: her delightful sauciness and her face – so dangerous to the man who looks at it – burn me.

Odes, 1.19

Parian marble from the Greek island of Paros was the most prized in the ancient world, producing a dazzlingly glittering, ultra-white stone when carved.

The satirist Juvenal was less rosy-tinted in his views of women. He said aristocratic women had as much stamina and aptitude when it came to sex as the most desirable prostitutes in Rome. Saufeia and Medullina were names that represented the oldest families in Rome:

Lenonum ancillas posita Saufeia corona provocat ac tollit pendentis praemia coxae; ipsa Medullinae fluctum crisantis adorat.

> **Saufeia casts her wreath aside and challenges the call-girls to a humping contest. She wins the prize but then gives up first place to Medullina, staring in admiration at those buttocks rising and falling like the waves of the sea.**

Medullina's name recalled the notorious Messalina, whose sexual appetite was the talk of Rome. She married her lover when her husband, Emperor Claudius, was away from Rome. She planned to overthrow Claudius and rule Rome with her new husband. When Claudius returned earlier than expected, she was executed, together with her lover.

Martial, a contemporary of Juvenal famous for his biting epigrams, was pretty graphic, too, about a prostitute he calls 'the girl from Cadiz'.

> **Tam tremulum crisat, tam blandum prurit, ut ipsum masturbatorem fecerit Hippolytum.**

> **She moves her buttocks so lithely; she invites sex so seductively that she made even Hippolytus turn to masturbation.**

The Latin for **masturbator**, you'll see, is identical: **masturbator**. In Greek myth, Hippolytus was a youth who resisted his stepmother's advances out of a pathological loathing of the female sex. He is the subject of a Euripides tragedy, *Hippolytus*, that inspired Racine's *Phèdre*.

Elsewhere, Martial described two men arriving one morning to have sex with Phyllis. The girl's Greek name suggests she was a prostitute and clearly in demand among the young men of the capital. The problem was that both men wanted to be first to make love. This was Phyllis's resourceful solution.

Promisit pariter se Phyllis utrique daturam et dedit:
ille pedem sustulit, hic tunicam.

Phyllis promised to give herself to each of them equally, and so she did: one lifted up her feet, the other her tunic.

Martial could be more romantic, as in this poem about Catulla – lovelier but therefore less attainable than anyone else:

O quam te fieri, Catulla, vellem
formosam minus aut minus pudicam.

Oh, Catulla, how I'd like you to become less beautiful, or less virtuous.

Martial wasn't always obsessed with sex and romance. Here, in a poem addressed to himself, he reflects on all the things that make for a happier life. He recommends good health, true friends and the avoidance of legal disputes, wine and women:

Nox non ebria, sed soluta curis,
non tristis torus, et tamen pudicus.

A night not fuddled with wine but free from worries,
a bed where fun reigns, and yet only with me.

Look out for the word *ebria* as in **nox ebria** – **drunken night**. It's where we get the word 'inebriated' from. The crime novelist Patricia Highsmith – often *ebria* herself – was fond of the line, **Dum non sobrius, tamen non ebrius: 'Be never quite sober, never quite drunk,'** as she translated it in *Deep Water* (1957). The word *sobrius* – sober – is derived from **se-** (**without**) and **ebrius** (**drunk**).

In Rome, Greek was the language of intimacy and love, as French was to Russian and English aristocrats of the nineteenth century. And the Greek city of Corinth was considered the most sexually thrilling place anywhere. In the following poem, Martial says Laelia should behave more seductively in bed – like the famous prostitutes of Corinth in the Temple of Aphrodite – if she is to emulate Lais, the most famous of them.

Tu licet ediscas totam referasque Corinthum, non tamen omnino, Laelia, Lais eris.

You may learn by heart all that Corinth has to teach and make it your own, but you'll never completely be a Lais, Laelia.

In the ancient world, the Corinthians were thought to be impossibly louche. They made easy money out of the toll fees charged for crossing the isthmus at Corinth. And they spent the proceeds on prostitutes. The ancient Temple of Aphrodite in Corinth was so packed with them that Aristophanes referred to sex as 'Corinthing'.

In St Paul's first letter to the Corinthians, he wrote, 'Neither fornicators, nor idolaters, nor adulterers, nor effeminate, nor abusers of themselves with mankind, nor thieves, nor covetous, nor drunkards, nor revilers, nor extortioners, shall inherit the kingdom of God. And such were some of you.'

Martial ends his poem with an invented, comic example from Homer's *Odyssey*, involving the poem's chaste heroine, Penelope. When her husband was snoring in bed, dreaming of past conquests, writes Martial, she knew exactly where to place her hand to get his attention.

'Sorry, Horatius, we won't need you after all for the bridge, or Herminius or Lartius – we've got Obesius instead'

Ed McLachlan's cartoon about Horatius at the Bridge. The soldier Horatius defended the Pons Sublicius in Rome from the Etruscan king Lars Porsena in the late 6th century BC. It inspired the poem *Horatius at the Bridge* by Thomas Babington Macaulay (1800–59).

5

Latin Jokes and Insults

At the beginning of *The Art of Poetry*, Horace tells a story that, he promises, will make anyone laugh: 'If a painter wanted to put a horse's head on a human neck, would you be able to keep your laughter in?'

Would you? I certainly would.

That's the thing about Roman jokes – they're not really very funny now. In 2008, when the late comic and *Bullseye* host Jim Bowen did an act based on the fourth-century AD Roman joke book ***Philogelos*** (**The Laughter Lover**), the jokes hadn't improved with age:

> A man complains that a slave he was sold had died.
>
> 'When he was with me, he never did any such thing!' replies the seller.

Did that really have them rolling in the aisles in the Colosseum?

Even if we don't find their jokes funny, the Romans gave us the furniture for our own comedy today. The language of modern humour is rooted in Latin. **Iocus** is Latin for **joke**; **facetus**, as in facetious, is Latin for **witty**; **ridiculus**, as in ridiculous, meant **laughable**.

Roman comic situations were similar to ours, too. Sex figures prominently. Cicero's list of the different kinds of Roman jokes – based on ambiguity, the unexpected, wordplay, understatement, irony, ridicule, silliness and pratfalls – is pretty close to any comparable modern list. The basic skeleton of several Roman jokes still lives on in some modern gags. The old story about Enoch Powell's visit to the barber – 'How should I cut your hair, sir?' 'In silence' – appears in the *Philogelos* joke book.

Both Iris Murdoch, in *The Sea, the Sea*, and Sigmund Freud told versions of the story recounted by Valerius Maximus, the first-century AD Roman writer:

> A Roman governor of Sicily met an ordinary resident in the province who was his spitting image. The governor was amazed at the likeness, since his father had never been to the province.
>
> 'But my father went to Rome,' the lookalike pointed out.

The Romans even came up with the Englishman, Irishman and a Scotsman template, although their equivalents were the bald man, the barber and the clever man – with the clever man the butt of the gags in the *Philogelos* joke book.

For all the shared infrastructure of our jokes, though, there are some drastic differences. To begin with, Terence's 161 BC play, *The Eunuch*, is familiar comic territory – it sounds like an episode of *Up Pompeii!*. A lusty, lovesick youth, Charea, pretends to be a eunuch to get close to Pamphila, an attractive slave-girl – nothing there to shock Frankie Howerd. But then, at the end of the play, Charea uses his eunuch disguise to rape Pamphila, before marrying her – not so funny.

In one of the most radical differences between then and now, it appears that the Romans laughed – and, like us, transcribed laughter as 'Ha-ha' – but they didn't smile. There are no Roman words for smiling, backing up the theory of the French historian, Jacques Le Goff (1924–2014), that smiling was an invention of the Middle Ages.

Our insults, too, owe a lot to the Romans. Some of the most famous, most elegant Roman orators and lyrical poets could be unprintably disgusting in their attacks. Roman comedy – and insults – had no limits when it came to sex and bodily functions.

As we've seen, Latin is a wonderfully concise language – and it makes for pithy, short insults. Here is Horace, attacking a show-off: **'Longos imitaris' – 'You pretend to be one of the big shots.'** Apuleius – a second-century AD philosopher and writer of the earliest surviving Latin novel in full – happily dipped his pen into the gutter. **'Foetorem extremae latrinae,'** he wrote – **'You smell like the worst kind of toilet.'**

Just as they do today, insults – when they weren't just plain obscene – accused people of being stupid and dull. Sallust, a famous first-century BC politician and historian, says of an enemy, 'His mind is one vast wasteland.'

Every sort of writer – poet, historian and playwright – put the boot in. The second-century BC playwright Plautus attacked someone by declaring, 'Oh, your words are so boring, by Hercules, that you're killing me.' 'You run back and forth with a stupid expression', wrote Petronius, 'like a mouse in a roasting pot.'

Persius, a first-century AD poet, also ripped into a tedious acquaintance: 'Are you still snoring? Is your slack head almost snapped on its stalk, with your face unzipped by the yawns earned in yesterday's debaucheries? Do you have any goals at all, or is there any point to your life?'

Just like Les Dawson and Eric Morecambe, Roman writers laid into nagging wives and brutal husbands. Juvenal, the first-century AD poet and satirist, wrote of some poor, put-upon husband, 'He moans like a hen who's being bitten by her husband.'

The poet Martial really hit rock bottom when he attacked an enemy, Manneia. 'Your lap-dog, Manneia, licks your mouth and lips: it always did like to eat shit.' Of another enemy, Martial said, 'You're an informer and a muckraker, a con-man wheeler-dealer, a c***-sucker and an educator in evil. I'm amazed, Vacerra, that, despite that, you're still broke.'

The Roman Empire is littered with so-called 'curse texts' – lead tablets where Romans attacked each other in inscriptions. Over 600 of them have been found. The most common insult of all is to write **Iuppiter te perdat** – **May Jupiter destroy you!**

There were defamation laws in ancient Rome, but they were relatively lax compared to our libel laws today. As well as damaging someone's reputation, you had to intend to damage someone's reputation in Rome to be successfully sued. In Britain today, being accidentally defamatory is no defence. But the perils of insults in Rome could still be literally deadly – as they were for Cicero, the great Roman writer.

A German academic, Martin Jehne, of Technische Universität Dresden, has recently put together a compilation of Latin insults. 'The famous speaker Cicero, when he defended his supporter Sestius,' says Jehne, Julius Caesar's biographer, 'did not shrink from publicly accusing [his rival Publius] Clodius of incest with his brothers and sisters.'

Here is Cicero, usually thought of as the father of Roman oratory, attacking a witness, Publius Vatinius, at the trial of Sestius: 'No one thinks you're worth his attention, his time, a vote, a place in society, or even the light of day.'

Transvestites are nothing new, either. Cicero really tore into his enemy, Clodius, for attending the **Bona Dea** (**Good Goddess**) festival, dressed as a woman, to seduce Pompeia, Julius Caesar's wife – the festival was women-only, so there was no way he could get in as a man. 'Take away his saffron dress, his tiara, his girly shoes and purple laces, his bra, his Greek harp,' said Cicero of Clodius, 'take away his shameless behaviour and his sex crime, and Clodius is suddenly revealed as a democrat.'

No one was off-limits to Cicero, which, in the end, was his downfall. He took the massive risk of attacking Mark Antony, a leading politician and general in first-century BC Rome. 'You assumed a man's toga and at once turned it into a prostitute's frock,' Cicero said of Mark Antony. 'At first you were a common rent boy; you charged a fixed fee and a steep one at that.'

Soon after Cicero delivered this insult, Mark Antony took power over Rome, along with Lepidus and Octavian (later the Emperor Augustus). Cicero had to pay the price for his insults – in 43 BC he had his head cut off. On Mark Antony's orders, he also had his hands – which had written the insults against him – cut off, and they were nailed, along with his head, on the **rostra** (a **speaking platform** – from where we get the word 'rostrum') in the Roman Forum.

If you didn't have your head cut off for insulting senior politicians or emperors, you were in danger of being exiled. Ovid, the great love poet, was exiled by the Emperor Augustus to the Black Sea for a decade for what he called **carmen et error – a poem and a mistake**. The poem is thought to be Ovid's ***Ars Amatoria* – The Art of Love** – which was considered obscene and an encouragement to adultery, in lines like this, on how to pick up girls: 'Let your hook always be cast; in the pool where you least expect it, there will be fish.'

Cancellation of comedians these days suddenly doesn't seem so brutal, when you consider the Roman alternative.

Flora, Goddess of Flowers, at Villa Arianna, Stabiae, near Pompeii.

6

Latin for Gardeners

If you're a gardener who hates Latin – who prefers to call a yellow foxglove **a yellow foxglove** rather than **Digitalis lutea** – you may find the collision of Latin and **flores** (**flowers**) a bit intimidating.

Latin is in fact extremely helpful for the study of plants – and makes it much easier. Learn several dozen Latin terms (often, in fact, derived from Greek), and suddenly you'll understand the colour, size, scent, prickliness, fruitiness and medicinal properties of more than 3,000 plants.

Forget-me-not may sound lovelier than **Myosotis sylvatica**; **love-in-a-mist** more romantic than **Nigella damascena**. But those pretty English names won't disclose as much information as the Latin does: **sylvatica** means **growing in woodlands**; **damascena** means **connected with Damascus**.

The other thing is that the Latin terms are internationally recognizable, following rules set down by the International Code of Botanical Nomenclature in 1952. Moving as it sounds, love-lies-bleeding won't mean much to an Icelandic gardener, but he'll immediately know what you mean if you call it **Amaranthus caudatus** (**with a tail**).

And you don't even have to cross the Atlantic to come up against this international confusion. A Scottish **bluebell** is a **harebell** in England and Wales but, in all three countries, it's known in Latin as **Campanula rotundifolia**.

The real genius of the Latin is that it defines a plant in just two words – unlike the rambling, English equivalents.

Carl Linnaeus was the eighteenth-century Swedish botanist who invented the two-word – or binomial – system. Before he came along, there were Latin words for flowers – but they were often long strings of words, clumsy to use and tricky to correlate. Under Linnaeus's system, plants with shared features were divided up into species, genus and family.

The species is the basic unit of classification for plants. If the species have enough characteristics in common, they are grouped together into a larger, more general category, the genus. And those genera are in turn grouped together into an even larger, more general category – families, such as bamboo or orchids.

Take the *Digitalis lutea*, or yellow foxglove. *Digitalis* comes from **digitus** (**finger**, because of the plant's long, curving shape). And *Digitalis* is the genus. And *Digitalis lutea* (from **luteus**, **yellow**) is the species name. Just at a glance, then, you know that **Digitalis purpurea**, the **purple foxglove**, comes from the same genus as – but is a different species from – *Digitalis lutea*. And they both belong to the same plant family – Scrophulariaceae. Helpfully, all plant family names end in -aceae.

In the same way, the **primrose** (**Primula vulgaris**) and the **cowslip** (**Primula veris**) both belong to the primula genus. The primrose, which flowers so early, gets its name from the Latin **prima rosa – first rose**; even if it isn't actually a rose.

Within a species, there's a further classification. The word 'subsp.' after the species name means 'subspecies', i.e. another group within the species group, as in *Acer negundo* subsp. ***mexicanum*** (**connected with Mexico**).

If the species name has '*var.*' (short for **varietas** – **variety**) in front of it, the plant has a slight variation in its botanical structure, like *Acer palmatum var.* ***coreanum*** (**connected with Korea**).

Finally, if the Latin plant name has a descriptive name or an English proper name after it, like Digitalis purpurea subsp. heywoodii 'Silver Fox' – it's a garden cultivar. In other words, the plant has been artificially cultivated for colour, smell or foliage. The special name given by the cultivator reflects that special quality.

On top of all this, the **forma** (**form** or **appearance**; '*f.*' for short) distinguishes minor variations like the colour of the flower, as in *Acer mono f.* **ambiguum** (**doubtful**). And a hybrid – marked with a multiplication sign – means a cross-between species, like *Hamamelis* x **intermedia** (**intermediate in colour, form or habitat**).

But, still, stick just to genus and species and you'll get a long way. As you learn more classical terms, wonderfully descriptive little stories emerge from those two brief words.

So, *Eucalyptus pulverulenta* comes from Greek and Latin. Eucalyptus is derived from the two Greek words, *eu* ('well') and *kalyptos* ('hidden'), after the calyx that hides the plant's flowers; while *pulverulenta* comes from **pulvis** (**dust**), because the plant has a grey, dusty patina to it.

You'll end up learning some exceptionally beautiful words. The genus *Oenanthe* comes from the Greek, meaning 'wine flower'. When the stems are crushed, they produce a scent that smells like wine (rather nicer than plants described as **zibethinus** – **as disgusting-smelling as a civet cat**). *Oenanthe* **fistulosa** (**hollow**), the tubular dropwort, is a native British wildflower, often found on marshy ground. Be careful, though: all *Oenanthes* are poisonous, and *Oenanthe* ***crocata*** (**saffron yellow**), or the hemlock water dropwort, is one of the most poisonous of all British plants.

There are charming classical stories behind plant names, too. Acanthus – the prickly-leaved plant that clusters around the top of Corinthian and Composite column capitals – comes from the Greek for thorn. So the simple stem, *acanth-*, means 'spiky, spiny or thorny', as in **acanthocomus** (**with spiny hairs on the leaves**) or **acanthifolius** – **spiky-leaved**, as in the spiky aster, **Carlina acanthifolia**. The word is in turn derived from the Greek nymph Acantha, who fought off a pass from randy Apollo, only to scratch him in the face in the process. The rejected god was so incensed that he turned her into the spiky Acanthus plant on the spot.

In an ideal world, it's best to know both the English and the Latin name, as is the case with the **snake's head fritillary (Fritillaria meleagris)**. With its bobbing flower head, this lovely wildflower, found in British meadows, does indeed look like a snake. The Latin tells a different story – **meleagris** means **spotted like a guinea fowl**. Once you know both animal stories, how could you fail to recognize something shaped like a snake's head, with guinea fowl spots? Again and again, it makes logical – and romantic – sense for plant lovers to become Latin lovers.

Sadly, this whole magical naming system is under threat. 250 years after Linnaeus came up with the binomial Latin naming system for flowers, botanists are junking their classics. The binomial system – where all plants are given a genus and a species name in Latin – is surviving. But another rule – that all botanists must register an official description of a newly discovered plant in Latin – was dropped.

After a 2011 vote at the International Botanical Congress, you can now describe your new discoveries – of plants, fungi and algae – in English. (New animals will still have to be described in Latin.) So it's bye-bye to lovely terms like **oleraceus** and **ramulosus**, and it's hello to unlovely translations like **used as a vegetable** and **twiggy**.

How silly – and illogical. Because Latin is a dead language, its definitions are set in stone. With living languages, you get constant development and blurred overlaps between different tongues: thus Franglais, a mangling of French and English, and Denglish, a mixture of German and English. With Latin, there's no wriggle room; no room for error, misunderstanding or bargaining over meaning between countries. That precision, in a root language shared by its descendant languages, is what botanists need when they're describing new plants.

Without Latin as the international botanical language, there are countless names for the same plant. So we gave *Digitalis* the charming, but vague, name of foxglove – thanks to the legend that foxes used the long, tubular flowers as gloves over their fingers to mask their pawprints on the henhouse door. The French call the foxglove *gant de Notre Dame*, meaning 'Our Lady's Glove', and the Irish call it a fairy's cap. Cue massive confusion at any botanical gathering – but for the wonderful unifying, defining power of Latin. All nationalities can then settle on the official name, *Digitalis*, to accompany those unclear slang names, alluring as they are.

Thank God there's no danger of surgeons changing the name of our bones yet. The humerus in the upper arm is still the humerus; the tibia is still next to the fibula. Again – just as with the plants – how helpful to have agreed terms across countries and languages.

If you break your leg on an Alpine skiing holiday, be grateful for the ease of saying you've broken your tibia, rather than trying to work out the French/German for 'the bigger, stronger bone below the knee'.

WHAT'S IN A NAME? – Latin Gardening Tips

Very often, the species – or the second of a plant's two Latin names – will give away where it's from, where it likes to be planted and what it'll look like when fully grown.

Geographical

borealis – northern
australis – southern (as in Australia)
orientalis – eastern (as in the Orient)
occidentalis – western

Planting Conditions

ammophilus – likes sandy places
salinus – keen on salt
monticolus – growing wild in the mountains

How It'll End Up Looking

scandens – a climber
repens – a creeper
nanus – dwarf
cyclops and titanus – enormous
orbicularis – flat and round, like a disc
mollis – soft, as in Alchemilla mollis
superciliaris – shaped like an eyebrow, as in the orchid Cypripedium x superciliare

PS Some Latin Pitfalls

Each adjective has a masculine, feminine and neuter form, even if they are similar. *Albus* is the masculine for white; *alba* the feminine; *album* the neuter. Also, there are often many different words meaning very nearly the same thing, particularly if it's a colour that Romans used a lot in their dyes. So **flavens**, **flaveolus**, **flavescens** and **flavidus** all mean **yellowish**. Only **flavus** means pure **yellow**.

7

Bathtime, Feasts and *La Dolce Vita*

Balnea, vina, Venus corrumpunt corpora nostra sed vitam faciunt.

Baths, wine and Venus corrupt our bodies but they're the things that make life good!

Corpus of Latin Inscriptions, 6. 15258

As this anonymous inscription shows, virtually free access to public baths was a crucial part of Roman life. Baths were heated (hence their popular name, **thermae – warm baths**) by an underground system. The great aqueducts brought clean water to baths in the capital and other cities throughout the empire.

The baths at Rome were enormous. When the Visigoths sacked the city in 410 AD, they were convinced the early third-century AD Baths of Caracalla (emperor from 198 to 217 AD) must have been the emperor's palace because they were so grand. The Baths of Caracalla are now used for public performances – including the Three Tenors concert at the Italian World Cup in 1990.

Still today at Wroxeter, the Roman fortress Viroconium in Shropshire, the biggest surviving structure is the towering wall of the baths.

Wroxeter is Shropshire's answer to Pompeii. The Roman city is the same size as Pompeii – 180 acres – though most of it lies tantalizingly unexcavated. In its time, Viroconium was the fourth largest city in Roman Britain, with 5,000 inhabitants.

Today, it's a staggering sight, with that towering section of the second-century baths dominating views in all directions. Here, at the outpost of the empire, they built **apodyteria** (**changing rooms**), **tepidaria** (**warm rooms**), **caldaria** (**hot rooms**) and a **frigidarium** (a **cold bath**) on a scale that puts any modern spa to shame. There was once a mighty forum and basilica, too – all a reminder that Roman Britain wasn't some dingy, colonial backwater but a really significant part of the empire that underpins Western civilization.

Tragically, after the Romans left Britain in 410 AD, lots of the buildings were looted for their stone. If you want to see where they ended up, just walk to the church of St Andrew's, Wroxeter, built out of Roman stone, with two enchanting Doric columns as gateposts. In a nearby garden, more columns are incorporated into a pretty little folly. Never have the stones of British history been so enchantingly arranged.

From the third century BC, rich aristocrats enjoyed bath suites in their town houses and country villas. By the time of Augustus, there were 170 public baths in Rome. At the height of their popularity, there were a thousand in Rome alone. They were part of the **commoda** (**perks**) the elite offered the masses – a pay-off for their dependence on patronage, now they'd lost the vote they'd enjoyed under the Republic.

Baths were as much a hallmark of Roman civilization across the empire as theatres were of Greek culture. Tacitus says they went down particularly well with the British chieftains:

> **Inde etiam habitus nostri honor et frequens toga. Paulatimque discessum ad delenimenta vitiorum, porticus et balinea et conviviorum elegantiam.**

Idque apud imperitos humanitas vocabatur, cum pars servitutis esset.

They even fell for our fashions and started wearing togas.
Little by little, they were drawn to things with a touch of sinfulness to them: drawing rooms, hot baths, elegant dinner parties.
In their naivety, they called all this civilization when it was all part of their servitude.

Tacitus, *Agricola*, 21.2

Baths could be rough places, too, as Seneca, working in an office above a public bath, wrote:

Adice nunc scordalum et furem deprensum et illum cui vox sua in balineo placet.

Now add to this the rough characters shouting at each other, the thief caught in the act, and that fellow who so enjoys hearing his own singing echo through the bathhouse.

Seneca, *Letters to Lucilius*, 56.1

The baths were gathering places for ordinary men and their families. As a rule, women and children bathed at different times from men.

Baths may have been sociable but there were pitfalls. Clothes were stolen. Seneca complained, too, about the noise from 'confectioners, sausage hawkers, cake-sellers, body-builders exercising with heavy lead weights, and those louts who cannonball into the pool, hitting the water with a deafening splash'. Bombing – the practice outlawed in swimming pools today – has a long history. All human life was there.

Emperors and plutocrats created ever grander baths to impress each other – and to continue the paternalistic role the empire had adopted towards the people.

But how did the baths actually work? In his novel, *Satyricon*, Petronius (27–66 AD) wrote about the process:

> **Itaque intravimus balneum, et sudore calfacti momento temporis ad frigidam eximus.**
>
> **And so we made our way into the bath and, after staying there till we ran with sweat, we rushed through to the cold plunge bath.**
>
> Petronius, *Satyricon*, 28.1–3

The bather, sweating from playing games or wrestling, would undress and leave his clothes in the **apodyterium** (**changing room**). He then entered the **sudatorium** (**steam room** or **sweating room**, from **sudor – sweat**) to continue the sweating process before he entered the **caldarium** – the **hot room with a hot plunge bath**. Here he sprinkled hot water on himself from a large tub and had all the sweat and grime scraped off his body by an attendant with a **strigilis** – a **strigil**, or **scraper**. He would then enter the **tepidarium** (**warm room**) to cool off gradually before taking a plunge in the **frigidarium** (**cold pool**).

In the *Satyricon*, two students go to dinner with their eccentric host just after he's had the full luxury treatment at the baths. He's been 'rubbed down with napkins of the finest wool before being wrapped in a scarlet cloak, deposited in his litter and carried off home'.

Bathers would often have a light snack or take advantage of the prostitutes who worked at the baths. Others might linger in the public halls for a chat over a glass of wine or read in the libraries until closing time. Sculptural masterpieces were installed by emperors in the baths, on mosaic pavements under coffered vaults, for people to enjoy. The Laocoön group, now in the Vatican, was discovered in the Baths of Trajan in Rome.

The baths, like the gym today, were health-giving. The satirist Juvenal ends a poem about the vanity of human wishes by recommending the best gift to ask from the gods.

Orandum est ut sit mens sana in corpore sano.

You should pray to have a healthy mind in a healthy body.

Juvenal, *Satires*, 10.356

Juvenal, as so often, coined an expression that survives today: *mens sana in corpore sano.*

In their dazzling marble grandeur, so unlike most homes, the baths must have made the people feel genuine beneficiaries of Rome's empire. Still, the water was only cleaned irregularly. The Emperor Marcus Aurelius thought the baths constituted a health risk: **'What does public bathing look like to you? Oil, nasty refuse, dirty water, everything disgusting.'**

You must compare them, though, with the stench of the streets caused by poor sanitation. The city occupied only 8 square miles but housed a million people when Augustus became emperor (27 BC) and five million when he died in 14 AD. To most Romans, the baths must have seemed a blissful retreat from the day's back-breaking toil.

The **cena** or **evening meal** was a central part of *la dolce vita* for Romans. Good company was at a premium:

Cenae fercula nostrae malim convivis quam placuisse cocis.

When it comes to the dishes I provide for dinner, I'd rather have the approval of my guests than the cooks.

Martial, *Epigrams*, 9.81.3

Breakfast (**ientaculum**) and **lunch** (**prandium** – as in post-prandial) tended to be light affairs – cold meals 'with no need for setting a table or washing the hands afterwards', according to Seneca.

Dinner came after the visit to the baths for exercise and relaxation. It took place in the mid-afternoon or a bit later in summer. The dinner varied according to personal tastes and circumstances. For most rich Romans, it was, as for Pliny the Elder, 'an elegant and moderate repast'.

Virgil described a lavish royal banquet given by Dido, Queen of Carthage, to welcome Aeneas and his fellow distinguished Trojan guests.

Conveniunt, stratoque super discumbitur ostro.

They assembled and lay down for the meal on purple coverlets.

Virgil, *Aeneid*, 1.700

Romans reclined at dinner, with their left elbow resting on a cushion. Only children sat down. Grown-ups lay down in an arrangement of three sloping couches around a square table. The central couch was taken by the host, with the place of honour on his immediate right. This explains the name **triclinium** (**place of three couches**) most often used for the dining room.

Juvenal complained about the size of the menu at some lavish dinners.

Quis fercula septem secreto cenavit avus?

Which of our grandfathers had a dinner in private, off seven courses?

Juvenal, *Satires,* 1. 94–5

In fact, grand dinners had *at least* seven courses – the **gustatio** (**hors d'oeuvre**), three entrées, two roasts and the **secundae mensae** (**pudding**).

Our picture of Roman dinners as orgies of consumption is a generalization based on greedy monsters like the Emperors Nero and Vitellius. That kind of dinner began at noon, with the drunken guests retiring to bed, says Juvenal, 'at an hour when our generals of old would be striking camp'. Dinners often did descend into excess:

Vomunt ut edant, edunt ut vomant.

They throw up in order to eat and eat in order to throw up.

Seneca, *Consolation to Helvia,* 10.3

Poets, particularly Horace, celebrated drunkenness. One of his most famous lines was

Nunc est bibendum.

Now we must drink.

In his *Epistles*, Horace wrote:

Quid non ebrietas dissignat?

What cannot be sorted out by drunkenness?

Also, in his *Epistles*, he said,

Nulla placere diu nec vivere carmina possunt, quae scribuntur aquae potoribus.

No poems written by water-drinkers can give pleasure for very long or live on.

Epp., 1.19.2–3

And, in his *Odes*, Horace declared,

Siccis omnia nam dura deus proposuit, neque mordaces aliter diffugiunt sollicitudines.

For God has put only obstacles in the way of teetotallers, and only wine can put gnawing worries to flight.

Odes, 1.18.3–4

It wasn't just Horace who praised drunkenness. Petronius declared,

Aquam foras, vinum intro.

Out with water; in with wine!

Sat., 52

Cenae could be very long, with professional buffoons and dancing girls providing entertainment between courses. Waiters were on hand, as the poet Lygdamus writes:

Cessas, o lente minister? Temperet annosum Marcia lympha merum.

Hey, get a move on, steward – you're dallying! This vintage wine needs some good Marcian water to dilute it!

Lygdamus, *The Tibullan Collection*, 3.6.57–8

Lygdamus is referring to fresh water supplied from the Marcian aqueduct.

Roman wine was blended with resin and pine pitch, and then sealed in **amphorae** (**jars**) with necks stoppered with cork or clay. A label dated the vintage by means of the name of the consul in whose year the amphora was sealed. A vintage that was **annosum** (**full of years**) was much prized.

The wine universally praised in Latin literature was the 'immortal Falernian', from the northern region of the Roman Campagna. This wine and its rivals were all heavy. No one drank it neat unless they wanted to become drunk very quickly – considered an uncivilized practice, best left to barbarians.

Not that great leaders didn't get smashed, too. The historian Quintus Curtius was shocked by Alexander the Great's order that Persepolis, the Persian capital, should be torched when he was drunk.

Tam praeclaram urbem a comissabundo rege deletam esse.

To think that a city so famous was laid in ruins by a king in his cups!

Curtius, *History of Alexander the Great*, 5.7.10

In the centre of the Roman dining room, there sat a **cratera** (**mixing bowl**). Wine was mixed with water in this and passed through a funnel-strainer to remove any impurities. It was then poured into the guests' **pocula** (**cups**). The usual ratio was three parts water to two parts wine. Wine was normally drunk mixed with water but, when taken **merum** (**neat**), could lead to drunken violence associated with barbarian tribesmen.

Dinners sometimes ended with a **comissatio** (**a ceremonial drinking match**). The **magister bibendi** (**master of drinking**) prescribed the number of cups of wine each guest should drink – downed in one – and in what order.

We don't know what was taken the next morning to ease a **crapula** (**hangover** – as in crapulous). Binge-drinkers drank 'the Thracian way', as Horace puts it – i.e. without any water on the table to detract from the full Bacchic experience.

The highlight of Petronius's novel *Satyricon* is 'Dinner with Trimalchio', a funny satire on the pretensions of Trimalchio, a rich, vulgar ex-slave. *Trimalchio in West Egg* was an alternative title F. Scott Fitzgerald considered for *The Great Gatsby*. Trimalchio was quite a wine snob:

> **Vinum vita est. Verum Opimianum praesto. Heri non tam bonum posui et multo honestiores cenabant.**
>
> **Wine is life. I'm giving you real wine from Opimius's consulship. I didn't serve wine as good as this yesterday and my dinner guests were a much better class of people.**
>
> Petronius, *Satyricon*, 34.25–7

Rich Romans like Horace were keen on fine wine. Here he tells Lyde, his Greek girlfriend, to get on with their own private party by fetching and opening a jar of Caecuban wine. This was one of Italy's finest wines, with a vintage that dates back many years to the days when Bibulus was consul.

Inclinare meridiem sentis, ac veluti stet volucris dies, parcis deripere horreo cessantem Bibuli consulis amphoram.

You're aware the afternoon is drawing on and, as if time that usually flies is standing still, you leave the wine jar lying there idly in the cellar, though it holds Caecuban wine stoppered when Bibulus was consul.

Horace, *Odes* 3.28.5–8

Pliny the Younger described a real dinner party where wine snobbery was indulged in by someone who didn't have the excuse of being nouveau riche like Petronius's fictional character.

Vinum etiam parvolis lagunculis in tria genera discripserat, non ut potestas eligendi, sed ne ius esset recusandi, aliud sibi et nobis, aliud minoribus amicis (nam gradatim amicos habet), aliud suis nostrisque libertis.

He had even put the wine into minuscule flasks, separated into three categories, not to let guests choose but to make it impossible for them to refuse what they were given. One of these was for himself and us, the second for his less important friends (he grades all his friends) and the third for those who had once been in his or our service.

Pliny, *Letters,* 2.6, 5–9

Pliny objected to his host's 'elegant economy', calling it 'a kind of stingy extravagance'. He added, with some self-congratulation, that when he had a dinner party, he invited guests to a meal together, 'not to make class distinctions'.

Such snobbery was common. Under Roman law, even seating in the theatre was organized according to social rank. Horace describes a lavish **epulae** (**dinner**) he enjoyed at the home of Nasidienus, a nouveau riche tycoon with an adventurous cook.

> **Nam cetera turba nos, inquam, cenamus avis, conchylia, piscis. adfertur squillas inter murena natantis in patina porrecta.**
>
> **For the rest of the crowd – that's to say, us – were dining on fowl, oysters and fish. Next a moray eel was served, outstretched on a platter, surrounded by swimming scampi.**
>
> Horace, *Satires*, 2.8.26–7; 42–3

The guests were treated to 'the disjointed limbs of a crane, sprinkled generously with salt and meal, and the liver of a white goose, fattened on rich figs, and the forelegs of hares torn off, to make more agreeable eating, blackbirds with burnt breasts and wood-pigeons without the rumps'.

Fish were caught in the bays west of Rome. The Mediterranean was swimming with shellfish, large and small. A particular favourite was made in Pompeii: **garum**, **fish sauce** prepared chiefly from **scomber** or mackerel. Gourmets like the wealthy Lucullus had **piscinae** (**fish ponds**) attached to their villas, where they stocked lampreys, mullet and other exotic fish. Cicero called these men **piscinatores** (**fish-pond fanciers**).

Produce was imported to Rome, via its sea port, Ostia, from every part of the empire: Spanish pickles to season eggs;

pork from Gaul; apples, pears and figs from Chios; dates from Egyptian oases; African lemons and pomegranates; Damascus plums. There was plenty of game, particularly wild boar, in the forests north of Rome, while endless cheeses, oil and vegetables were available across Italy.

Such luxury was only for the rich. Martial described a more typical evening meal: 'Sliced eggs with lizard fish for your hors d'oeuvre; a young goat, together with meatballs and some chicken; beans and sprouts for vegetables; and ripe apples for dessert.' 'There will be jokes,' he reassured his guests, 'but nothing unpleasant, free speech that you needn't dread the next morning, and not a word you would wish unsaid.'

For the idle rich, who could afford to escape the oppressive heat of the capital and have fun among their own kind, the fashionable town of Baiae near Naples was much prized.

Cicero, defending a young man on a murder charge, cites the list of 'depravities' he is accused of, before showing that the woman behind the accusation, the aristocratic lady Clodia, was herself an eager participant in all of these activities – including going to Baiae.

Accusatores quidem libidines, amores, adulteria, Baias, actas, convivia, comissationes, cantus, symphonias, navigia iactant.

The prosecution go on about debauchery, love affairs, adultery, Baiae, and its beach, banquets and parties, singing, music and boat-trips.

Cicero, *Pro Caelio*, 35.9–11

The name of the town became synonymous with luxurious and immoral living, with partying on and off the water from dawn till dusk. As Horace said, **'No bay in the world outshines lovely Baiae's.'**

At Baiae, the bored wives of senators could leave their husbands to their civic responsibilities in Rome, escaping the stifling propriety of life in the capital, where they had to behave like Victorian wives, for unsupervised fun with young men.

Different parts of the Empire were associated with different practices – including sexual ones. You see it in this poem about Clodia, a former lover of Caelius. When she brought a murder charge against him, he made a cruel pun about her, recorded by the distinguished advocate Quintilian:

> **In triclinio Coa, in cubiculo Nola.**
>
> **In the dining-room, she was Coan; in the bedroom, Nolan.**
>
> Quintilian, *Training of the Orator*, 8.6.52

'Coan' means she wore expensive silk dresses imported from the Dodecanese island of Cos – the height of fashion for ladies of wealth. Silk was also sheer and transparent, meaning she would have attracted the male gaze as part of her strategy. 'Nolan' refers to the little country town of Nola, also near Naples, looked down on as provincial by the rich ladies of the capital.

Caelius is saying she may have looked the height of fashion but her behaviour in bed wouldn't have disgraced a no-nonsense country girl. For all her airs and graces, she was no different from a common prostitute.

It wasn't just prostitutes who misbehaved. Customers in one Pompeii dining room were so naughty that this notice was painted on the walls:

Lascivos voltus et blandos aufer ocellos coniuge ab alterius; sit tibi in ore pudor utere blandiis odiosaque iurgia differ si potes, aut gressus ad tua tecta refer.

No ogling of a fellow-diner's wife, please, with flattering glances; keep your remarks within the bounds of decency.

If you can, be agreeable company, and avoid quarrels that leave a bad taste. If you can't, kindly return to your own home.

*Notizie degli Scavi di Antichita (*1927), 93–4

I'm afraid manners weren't much better at the circus – our next subject.

"I suspect match-fixing here."

8

Bread, Circuses and Gladiators

Duas tantum res anxius optat, panem et circenses.

The people long for two things only, bread and games in the Circus.

Juvenal, *Satires*, 10.80–1

This is the context of Juvenal's famous 'bread and circuses' line. In the early second century AD, Juvenal was lamenting the way the people of Rome gave up their right to vote on all important issues in return for entertainment in the Great Circus – primarily chariot-racing – and the monthly distribution of free grain, imported from Africa and Egypt.

The emperors knew their popularity at home depended on the *annona* (the year's grain supplies from the provinces) and on regular entertainment. Grain arrived at Rome's harbours of Ostia and Portus, from where it was brought up the Tiber to the capital by barge and stored in huge granaries.

In Ostia, as a mark of its importance, there was a temple to Annona Augusta, the goddess of imperial supplies, linking the empire's bounty with the emperor, Rome's supreme patron.

By the time of the Emperor Claudius (41–54 AD), the Romans had at least one day of holiday for every working day. There were 159 days of leisure, of which 93 were given over to **ludi** (**games**). The rest were divided between gladiatorial combats or **munera** (**gifts**), paid for by magistrates or the emperor himself, and festivals. This entertainment – together with the public banquets held to celebrate important dates in the calendar, a distinct improvement on their normal diet – was seen by the people of Rome as the essence of *la dolce vita*.

The historian Tacitus characterized the early success of Emperor Augustus as well-judged bribery – a shrewd political move before he went on 'to absorb the functions of the senate, the magistrates and the law itself'.

> **Ubi militem donis, populum annona, cunctos dulcedine otii pellexit.**
>
> **He won over the army with bonuses, the people with cheap food and the entire citizen body with the delightful gift of peace.**
>
> Tacitus, *Annals*, 1.2.21–2

Before Augustus became emperor, the people were weary of civil war and the excesses of republican government under corrupt aristocrats. Emperors were keen to keep the masses happy – thus the need to feed and entertain their subjects.

Not everyone agreed. Pliny the Younger disapproved of the chariot races in the Great Circus, in the valley between the Aventine and Palatine hills (used more recently for Mussolini's grandiose exhibitions).

> **Quo magis miror tot milia virorum tam pueriliter identidem cupere currentes equos, insistentes curribus homines videre.**
>
> **So it amazes me all the more that so many thousands of grown men have so childish a passion for watching horses galloping and men who drive them, standing in chariots, time and time again.**
>
> Pliny the Younger, *Letters*, 9.6.5–7

Chariot racing was the most popular of the games provided for the people of Rome. 300,000 spectators were accommodated on marble or wooden seats, with standing places in the top tier. Each race was seven laps (roughly five miles in total) and lasted about 15 minutes. Racing went on for several days at a stretch. As in the sequence in *Ben-Hur* (1959), pile-ups were frequent, despite the drivers' skill – though Ben-Hur's Roman enemy wouldn't have been allowed to sport scythed chariot wheels.

'What are you staring at? Haven't you seen a 4x4 before?'

Still, carnage, involving man and beast, was part of the attraction. There were teams of two, three or (most commonly) four horses. Betting was heavy, with a keen eye for the talent of the drivers and the condition of the highly trained horses.

Victory depended on the skill with which the charioteers handled the two sharp turns at the end of the **spina** (**the long, straight course**). They could only overtake the team ahead by shaving the cone-shaped **meta** (**turning-post**) on the inside.

The drivers belonged to four **factiones** (**stables**), increased to six by the Emperor Domitian but only for a short while. Each had a different colour: **white** (**albata**), **green** (**viridis)**, **red** (**russata**) and **blue** (**veneta**). The drivers wore **shirts** (**panni**) in the colour of their stable.

Totam hodie Romam circus capit, et fragor aurem percutit, eventum viridis quo colligo panni.

All Rome is inside the Circus today and a roar strikes my ear, which tells me the Greens have won the race.

Juvenal, *Satires*, 11.197–8

Juvenal approved of letting younger men attend the races 'with classy girls at their side' – a reminder that the Circus attracted a wide range of spectator.

The biographer of the Caesars, Suetonius, said the emperors Caligula, Nero and Domitian supported the Greens. Vitellius, Caracalla and Justinian supported the Blues. Nero always wanted to drive in a four-horse chariot race in the Circus. This was described by the aristocratic historian Tacitus as 'a disgusting passion', since the upper classes regarded public performance as demeaning. Pliny couldn't understand the appeal of these events for 'serious individuals who wasted days on end in the idlest of occupations'.

Each *factio* maintained a large number of saddlers, grooms, trainers, doctors and veterinary surgeons. The annual Palio in Siena comes closest to the intense rivalry and danger of these *ludi* but hardly matches the scale or frequency of the Roman games.

Most charioteers died in one of these 'bloody shipwrecks' at an early age, and very few managed to retire at the height of their fame. One of them, Diocles, quit the Circus with a fortune of 35 million sesterces, the accumulated property qualification of 35 senators, having won 1,462 victories. The faces of these top sportsmen were painted on the walls of houses all over Rome.

One epitaph records the successful career of a charioteer who drove for the Reds and then for the Purples under

Emperor Domitian, who created the short-lived purple and gold *factiones*. A Greek and former slave, who like most successful drivers eventually won his freedom, he left behind a loving wife.

Dis manibus Epaphroditus, agitator factionis russatae, vicit CLXXVIII, et ad purpuream libertus vicit VIII. Beia Felicula fecit coniugi suo bene merenti.

To the departed spirit of Epaphroditus: as charioteer of the Red stable, he won 178 victories and, of the Purple stable, as a freedman, eight. His wife, Beia Felicula, set up this memorial to her well-deserving husband.

Corpus of Latin Inscriptions, 6.10048

The excitement people previously sought in politics was now found, under the Caesars, in the Circus. The Circus factions replaced the old political parties, and the presiding emperor the consuls of the Republic.

The emperors were shrewd in their political use of the Circus. They made the people feel they shared their values and identified with them. They showered sweets and money on the people during the day. At the end of the day, they laid on an **epulum (public banquet**) for the crowd.

The emperor was seen as the source of all this entertainment. His arrival – with the imperial family – to begin proceedings was pure political theatre, stirring happiness and national pride in the appreciative spectators. Ovid gave a good feel of a day at the games.

Spectatum veniunt, veniunt spectentur ut ipsae; ille locus casti damna pudoris habet.

They come to watch and they come to be watched themselves; it's not a place where a girl holds on to her virtue for long.

Ovid, *Art of Love,* 1.99–100

Ovid said you should go to the theatres of Rome for new romance. 'That's where to find a girl to love,' he said, 'or one to have fun with, or one to touch just once, or one you want to keep.'

On the other hand, the chariot-racing in the Circus is where to take your long-term girlfriend. There you can sit beside her and rub your leg against hers as much as you like, brushing any specks of dust, real or imaginary, from her dress.

And always support her team if you want to get lucky:

Cuius equi veniant facito studiose requiras nec mora, quisquis erit cui favet illa, fave.

Make sure you ask carefully whose horses are coming up to the starting boxes, and the moment you learn which charioteer she supports, make him your favourite, too.

Ovid, *Art of Love,* 1.145–6

Romans loved victorious horses, as well as their jockeys. These words were discovered on a mosaic pavement in the baths at Numidia, north Africa: the proprietor of the baths, Pompeianus, declared his affection for the horse Polydoxus.

Vincas, non vincas, te amamus, Polydoxe!

Whether you win or lose, we love you, Polydoxus!

Recueil de Constantine (1880)

Another celebrated horse, Victor, lived up to his name on 429 occasions.

Horses were bought in the stud farms of Greece, Italy and Africa but mostly in Spain. Put into training from the age of three, they were competing in chariot races by five. Each of them had its own pedigree and list of triumphs. The best were celebrated throughout the empire, like an ancient Shergar or Red Rum.

The **agitatores** (**drivers**) won even greater glory from fans. But archaeology shows that their best horses, too, had their names incised on the rim of earthen lamps and became household names all over the Roman world.

Incidentally, the standard British rail gauge – 4ft 8½ inches – still mirrors the specification for a Roman war chariot. That figure, the Romans thought, reflected the size of a horse's bottom, with a little wriggle room on either side. The first Victorian trains were built to the same width as horse-drawn wagons; they, in turn, were designed to fit the ruts left in the roads by Roman chariots. As our bottoms grew bigger, those seats grew more uncomfortable. Next time you're tightly packed into the 5.37 from Waterloo, you know who to blame: the Ben-Hurs of Roman Londinium.

The Ancient Greeks invented the theatre – from the Greek **theatron**, a **watching place**. They also came up, in 465 BC, with the **backdrop** or **skene** – thus our word 'scene'. In 425 BC, a **proskenion** – a **low-slung portico** – was added in front of the skene; thus our proscenium arch.

The idea of the dramatic plot-reveal is Greek; as is the **deus ex machina**. The words are Latin – **god from the machine** – meaning the late arrival of a deity in a play, or a sudden revelation that saves the day. But the expression ultimately comes from the Greek, **mechane**, for the **crane** that allowed an actor to fly like a god.

Still, the Romans invented the amphitheatre – the theatre that goes all **around** (**amphi** in Greek). The most famous Roman architect Vitruvius (*c.* 80 BC–*c.* 15 BC), writing under Augustus, coined the word 'amphitheatre' to describe the theatre first introduced by Curio the Younger, a political friend of Julius Caesar, 130 years before.

In quibus civitatibus non sunt gymnasia neque amphitheatra.

Cities in which there are no gymnasia or amphitheatres.

Vitruvius, *On Architecture*, 1.7.1

To honour his dead father, Curio had two big, identical, wooden theatres constructed for his funeral. Their curves touched but were set back to back for two separate performances. At noon, he had his engineers turn the two theatres on their axes and come face to face to form an oval. The amphitheatre was born.

Under Augustus, amphitheatres were built in stone rather than wood. As Suetonius said of Augustus,

Iure sit gloriatus marmoream se relinquere, quam latericiam accepisset.

He could rightly boast that he found Rome a city of brick and left it a city of marble.

Suetonius, *Divus Augustus – 'Divine Augustus'*, 28

Amphitheatres were used for gladiatorial combats. As early as 160 BC, these bouts attracted huge crowds. Other athletes were so gripping that spectators once abandoned a comedy by Terence in a neighbouring theatre to watch 'spellbound' a **tightrope walker** (**funambulus**) performing next door.

The most famous amphitheatre – and still the biggest in the world – is the Colosseum, begun under the Emperor Vespasian in 72 AD and finished in 80 AD under his successor Titus.

Martial celebrated the new building, originally known as the 'Flavian Amphitheatre', after the Flavian emperors who ruled from 69 to 96 AD. The Flavian dynasty followed the childless Nero in 69 AD, after a year of civil war. The title 'Colosseum' derived from the new building's proximity to a colossal statue of Nero, transformed by Vespasian into a statue of the Sun.

Martial said the Colosseum would eclipse all the other wonders of the world, such as the Hanging Gardens of Babylon and the Temple of Diana at Ephesus.

> **Omnis Caesareo cedit labor Amphitheatro unum pro cunctis fama loquetur opus.**
>
> **Every work of architecture yields to Caesar's amphitheatre; fame will speak of a single building to eclipse all others.**
>
> Martial, *Book of Spectacles*, 1.7–8

The Colosseum played host to the **venationes**, **animal hunts** that provided an interlude between killings of gladiators by gladiators. Martial praised the **bestiarius** (**beast-fighter**) Carpophorus, whose hunting skills surpassed those of the hero Meleager, destroyer of the mythical Calydonian boar. Carpophorus, a darling of the crowd, enjoyed great fame.

> **Stravit et ignota spectandum mole leonem, Herculeas potuit qui decuisse manus, et volucrem longo porrexit vulnere pardum.**

He laid low a lion whose size was beyond anything the arena had witnessed before, a beast that could have been a match for mighty Hercules, and stretched out a swift-footed leopard on the sand with a raking wound.

Martial, *Book of Spectacles,* 15. 5–7

These men brought a change from the spectacle of animal fights (buffalo against rhinoceros; tiger against lion). They fought the beasts, armed with hunting spears and burning torches to balance the odds. Red cloths were waved in front of bulls and their lunges avoided by deft feints, as in Spanish bullrings today. The animals were kept below the arena in cages. From there, they were driven into lift shafts in the labyrinth of underground corridors and hoisted through those trapdoors into the blinding sunlight and noise of the arena to face a bloody death.

For many years, the Colosseum was neglected and forlorn, home to plenty of Rome's cats. But it has recently been the subject of a two-year restoration programme. Conservators unearthed the 60 lift shafts used to hoist lions, tigers and other predators through those arena trapdoors.

One of the highlights of the Colosseum was the flooding of the arena to host a mock **naumachia** or **sea battle**.

Hic modo terra fuit. Non credis? Specta, dum lassant aequora Martem: parva mora est, dices, 'Hic modo pontus erat.'

Land was here recently. You don't believe me? Look, until the waters tire the war-god: in no time at all, you'll be saying, 'The sea was here recently.'

Martial, *Book of Spectacles,* 24.4–6

Augustus first made this transformation, flushed with the success of the sea battle of Actium in 31 BC that broke the power of Antony and Cleopatra. Emperor Trajan perfected the system of water engineering in the new Colosseum. Its oval arena was 94 yards long and 59 yards wide, enclosing an area of 38,000 square feet, accommodating 50,000 spectators. Built of blocks of hard travertine stone from quarries near modern Tivoli, the Colosseum's four-storeyed walls were 62 yards high.

On very sunny days, if the emperor wanted, a vast awning sheltered the spectators and combatants, operated by sailors from the fleet headquarters at Misenum.

Seneca once went to the amphitheatre during the lunch-hour interlude, expecting 'some light and amusing entertainment', only to witness what could only be called 'murder, pure and simple'.

> **Mane leonibus et ursis homines, meridie spectatoribus suis obiciuntur.**
>
> **In the morning, men are thrown to the lions and bears; at midday, they are thrown to their devoted spectators.**
>
> Seneca, *Letters to Lucilius,* 7.4

The victims were robbers, murderers and arsonists, **condemned to death by the sword** (**ad gladium damnati**) on the sand of the arena. Men were killed without a weapon to defend themselves. The butchery lasted until they all died.

Before these fights, other victims were mauled to death by wild beasts released from the depths of the arena. A mosaic from Tripolis in North Africa shows one criminal being wheeled out, bound to a vertical pole, to be torn apart by a leopard (Aurigemma, *Mosaici*, 182).

In August 2021, the bronze key handle for a grand Roman townhouse was discovered in the centre of Leicester. It showed an unarmed barbarian grappling with a lion, with four naked young men cowering below. This was the first evidence that lions were imported to Roman Britain for the execution of captives in public spectacles.

York was home to some of the most savage gladiatorial contests the Roman Empire ever saw. In 2010, archaeologists announced that the world's best-preserved Roman gladiator cemetery had been discovered in Driffield Terrace, a street of smart period homes in the west of York. Among the 80 skeletons buried 3 feet below the well-heeled residents' gardens there was one poor gladiator with a large bite mark, thought to be courtesy of a bear, tiger or lion, sustained in York's bloody arena.

Most of the skeletons had much bigger sword-arm muscles than on their shield arm, after a lifetime of weapons training. Some had weapon injuries, healed and unhealed. Many had been decapitated. Others had hammer blows to the head – a deadly mark also seen in the less well-preserved gladiator cemetery in Ephesus, Turkey.

The finds showed the intense respect shown to gladiators, treated with the awe today's football stars command. 14 of them were buried together with grave goods – treasure and household items – to take with them to the next world.

The most impressive resting place belonged to a tall man, aged between 18 and 23, buried in an oval grave in the third century. He was killed, it appears, by several sword blows to the neck. Alongside him were the remains of substantial joints of meat, including at least four horses, a cow and a pig – possibly eaten at his funeral.

The discovery is an extremely rich and rare one, dating throughout practically the whole time the Romans were in Britain. The gladiators' skeletons date from the first to the fourth century AD; i.e. just before the Romans gave up their British outpost in 410 AD and headed back to Italy, as their empire collapsed around them.

It has always been known that York was one of the most important cities in Roman Britain. It was founded in 71 AD by the Romans, who made it the capital of the northern province of Britannia Inferior. York wasn't just a minor provincial outpost. The Emperor Hadrian – who built his wall north of York – held court there, as did the emperors Septimius Severus and Constantius I, who died in 306 AD in the city.

Such a crucial city needed powerful fortification; York's fortress covered 50 acres in the heart of the city. Today, York Minster stands only yards from those Yorkshire gladiators' final resting place.

We say Yorkshire gladiator, and yet these gladiators, like most gladiators across the Empire, were particularly strong slaves who'd been imported to the great Roman cities. The skeletons in York are very robust and taller than average. Tests on their teeth enamel link them to several Roman provinces, including North Africa, a major recruitment ground for gladiators.

In 1901, the so-called 'ivory bangle lady' was discovered buried in another Roman cemetery in York's Sycamore Terrace, by the banks of the River Ouse.

Aged between 19 and 23, she wore impressive ivory bracelets from Africa and jet bangles from Whitby. Analysis of her skull and her teeth revealed that she, too, came from north Africa. In one Roman cemetery in York, 11 per cent of the bodies were found to be of North African descent. These Africans were thoroughly absorbed into everyday Roman Yorkshire life. The bangle lady was not only well-off, but she must have spoken Latin, too. Buried with her was the inscription:

Soror ave vivas in deo.

Goodbye, sister. May you live in God.

The most famous gladiator of all, Spartacus – immortalized by Kirk Douglas in the 1960 film – was a humble slave from Thrace (roughly modern Bulgaria).

Spartacus led 73 fellow slave gladiators in the biggest rebellion in Rome's history, building his rebel group up to a 70,000-strong force that nearly destroyed Rome before he was killed in 71 BC. His army of slaves, trained as gladiators, was strikingly successful against Roman legions. It only lost because, in the end, it was hopelessly outnumbered. The mass crucifixion of the survivors, all the way from Capua to Rome, was a terrible warning, but also a measure of the fear they inspired as professional fighters.

It's surprising there weren't more rebellions, given the horrific life gladiators led. Yes, they were given good rations. But they were only being fattened up for death. All they had ahead of them were those damp graves under the patios of Driffield Terrace.

Even the top gladiators that survived early bouts were bound to face the final, fatal knockout one day. And they knew very well what fate awaited them. Thus their cry before battle:

Ave, Imperator, morituri te salutamus.

Hail, Emperor, we who are about to die salute you.

The decision whether they lived or died lay with the **editor**, a sort of **judge** – from where we get the word 'editor'. Contrary to popular wisdom, if the editor wanted to spare the gladiator, he gave the thumbs-down sign, allowing the gladiator to live to fight another day. A thumbs-up meant death.

These judges knew how to play a crowd: neither they nor their bosses, the emperors, were merciful for ever. **Oderint dum metuant – Let them hate me as long as they fear me** – was the catchphrase of the Emperor Caligula.

And the best way to instil fear and awe among the citizens was by the public, mass slaughter of gladiators – the strongest men in the Empire. It all made for riveting spectator sport for the 50,000-strong audience. Invariably it was a fight to the death, with each gladiator fighting toe to toe.

The writer Statius described a Roman swordfight, a desperately scary, all-in struggle for survival: 'And now shield clashed with shield, shield boss bounced against shield boss, sword threatened sword, foot tangled with foot, spearpoint with spearpoint.' The riveting spectacle was so popular that it spread across the Empire.

At the end of the fourth century AD, Augustine wrote about a young man, Alypius, who was dragged along to the amphitheatre by friends and became an instant convert.

> **Spectavit, clamavit, exarsit, abstulit inde secum insaniam, qua stimularetur redire, non tantum cum illis a quibus abstractus est, sed etiam prae illis et alios trahens.**
>
> **He became a spectator, shouting out, on fire with passion, and left, a victim of the madness that would drive him to go back once more, not only with the friends who had brought him there in the first place, but even without them, drawing others to join him.**
>
> Augustine, *Confessions*, 6.8

And now, thanks to this extraordinary discovery in York, or Eboracum, as the Romans called it, we can see that the sport's tentacles reached right up to the Empire's northern fringes.

The gladiator fights started early in the morning and continued all day without any intermission (until 61 BC, when a lunch break was set up – for the spectators).

There were all sorts of fights to keep the punters happy. The **equites** (**horsemen**) opened the show, riding on white horses, fighting with light weapons, protected only by small, golden helmets. The **provocatores** (**challengers**) fought with visored helmets, a loincloth (like all gladiators), a greave (or leg protector) and a breastplate. No other gladiators had any type of protective armour on their chest. The Thraex (or Thracian) had a large, rectangular shield and a short, curved **sica** (**sword**). The *hoplomachus* (a gladiator dressed to resemble an ancient Greek hoplite) depended on a thrusting spear. The **retiarius** (**netman)** is the most familiar figure – armed with a trident, he used a net to trap his opponents.

But, whatever the level of protection, the outcome was inevitable – a particularly gruesome death. If another gladiator didn't get you, the beasts did. The animals the gladiators faced weren't rundown circus pets. They were ferocious beasts, imported from the four corners of the Empire, which stretched right down from Hadrian's Wall all the way south into the wilds of north Africa. The bite mark on that poor gladiator in Eboracum could have come from an African lion or a Turkish bear, brought across the Empire at huge expense to kill the poor Spartacuses of Yorkshire.

The gladiators' appeal to women was understandable. Virtually naked, with an athletic, muscular body and known to be available for sex, the gladiator appears regularly in graffiti as **suspirium puellarum** (**the heart-throb of the girls** – *Corpus of Latin Inscriptions*, 4.4342).

Gladiators were so renowned and admired that they became objects of popular culture. In this passage, the vulgar freedman Trimalchio boasts to the guests at the dinner he is giving. He says the heavy cups they are drinking from are studded with jewels and illustrate scenes from a renowned contest between rival gladiators, Petraites and Hermeros.

> **Nam Hermerotis pugnas et Petraitis in poculis habeo, omnia ponderosa.**
>
> **And I've got scenes from the fight between Hermeros and Petraites on my cups, and every cup is heavy.**
>
> Petronius, *Satyricon*, 52.6–8

As well as drinking cups, lamps and precious glass jugs depicted scenes from the arena.

As the descendants of Mars, Romans admired gladiators as the embodiment of courage, prowess and disdain for danger. But they remained ambivalent figures for Roman society, inspiring admiration, fame, humiliation, contempt and fear.

In his comic masterpiece, Petronius gives an insight into the process of becoming a gladiator. The terrible oath shows how desperate they were, whether they were slaves or impoverished freedmen.

> **In verba Eumolpi iuravimus: uri, vinciri, verberari ferroque necari; tanquam legitimi gladiatores domino corpora animasque religiosissime addicimus.**
>
> **We swore an oath to obey Eumolpus: to suffer burning, bondage, flogging, and death by the sword; as though we were regular gladiators, we surrendered ourselves most solemnly, body and soul, to our master.**
>
> Petronius, *Satyricon*, 117.17–19

The 'master' was the grim figure of the **lanista**, a **professional manager of gladiators**. He would acquire, train and rent out gladiators, calculating, like a modern boxing manager, exactly when each one was ready for a particular contest.

Peter Ustinov's genial *lanista* in Stanley Kubrick's *Spartacus* (1960) groans wonderfully when Spartacus is chosen by a party of dissolute aristocrats to fight to the death for their pleasure. He knows his best gladiator is worth a small fortune to him – and may not survive the encounter.

In fact, the *lanista* was a far less savoury figure than Ustinov's character. They were often compared with the similar-sounding **lanius** (**butcher**) and **leno** (**pimp**), because they traded brutally in human flesh for profit.

By the time of the Emperor Caligula, who ruled from 37 to 41 AD, mime, a kind of farce, was the most popular entertainment, replacing plays. **Pantomimi** and **histriones** (**actors**, as in 'histrionic', and **ballet-dancers in mimes**) were idolized by the crowd. Even emperors were forced to acknowledge their popularity, admitting them to their courts as private entertainers.

A favourite mime subject in Rome's theatres had become the life and crucifixion of a notorious bandit named Laureolus. In this passage, Martial records how a condemned man was substituted for the actor playing Laureolus and actually crucified in the arena, where he was also savaged by a wild bear.

Nuda Caledonio sic viscera praebuit urso non falsa pendens in cruce Laureolus.

So Laureolus, hanging from a real cross, offered his naked flesh to the Caledonian bear.

Martial, *Book of Spectacles*, 7.3–4

The Emperor Domitian knew that a public used to the cruelties of the amphitheatre would enjoy it. The *Laureolus* remained popular for two centuries because of the ferocity of the bandit during his life and the hideous justice inflicted on him.

The most famous actor in first-century AD Rome was called Paris. He alerted Nero to a supposed plot by his mother, Agrippina, to seize the throne from him.

A grateful Nero decided to give Paris the status of a free man. The nobility, who regarded actors as immoral wastrels, objected violently. The historian Tacitus, himself a senator, shared the patrician disgust at Nero's love of acting and music and his desire to perform on stage before the urban population.

Nec multo post ereptus amitae libertus Paris quasi iure civili, non sine infamia principis cuius iussu perpetratum ingenuitatis iudicium erat.

Not long afterwards, supposedly on legal grounds, his aunt had her patronage of her freedman Paris taken away. This reflected badly on the emperor's reputation, since it was on his instruction that Paris was pronounced free-born.

Tacitus, *Annals*, 13.27. 22–4

Nero's love of performance fed into the legend that in 64 AD he fiddled – on a lyre or *cithara* – while Rome burned. The anecdote was told by the historians Suetonius and Cassius Dio long after Nero died.

Hoc incendium e turre Maecenatiana prospectans laetusque 'flammae', ut aiebat, 'pulchritudine' Halosin Ilii in illo suo scaenico habitu decantavit.

Viewing the conflagration from the tower of Maecenas and exulting, as he said, in 'the beauty of the flames', he sang the whole of *The Sack of Troy* in his regular stage costume.

Suetonius, *Life of Nero*, 38

Nero's mother, Agrippina, avenged herself on her accusers, including one called Atimetus, as far as she could. But such was the hold that Paris had on Nero that he remained untouchable, much to her frustration.

De Atimeto supplicium sumptum, validiore apud libidines principis Paride quam ut poena adficeretur.

Atimetus was executed but Paris played too important a role in the emperor's debauched practices to be punished.

Tacitus, *Annals*, 13.22.27–9

So an actor was able to survive the hatred of the most powerful woman in the empire. Still, Paris was eventually executed by Nero as a dangerous rival.

Under the Emperor Domitian, over 20 years later, another hugely popular actor, also named Paris, met a similar end after seducing the emperor's wife.

Just as Helen of Troy was forgiven by her husband for loving the original Paris, Prince of Troy, so Domitia Augusta, Domitian's wife, was restored as the emperor's wife and imperial consort. As Virgil had put it a hundred years earlier:

Omnia vincit Amor: et nos cedamus Amori.

Love conquers everything; let us give in to love, too.

Eclogues, 10.69

Early Christians were massacred in arenas all over the empire. They were thought to be proponents of a **'deadly superstition'** and **'hated for their depravity'** (**exitiabilis superstitio; per flagitia invisos** – Tacitus, *Annals*, 15.44. 9 and 12). They were accused of **'a debased superstition carried to excess'** (**superstitionem pravam, immodicam** – Pliny, *Letters*, 10.96.42) and **'a strange and wicked superstition'** (**superstitionis novae ac maleficae** – Suetonius, *Life of Nero*, 16.2).

The Christian apologist Tertullian (155–220 AD) said Christians were so hated, especially in the towns of the East, that they were made scapegoats for any natural disaster – 'earthquake, famine or plague'. Thus the popular cry:

Christianos ad leonem!

[Send] the Christians to the lion!

Tertullian, *Apology*, 40

Suetonius said the bookish emperor Claudius, who wrote a history of the Etruscans, made a habit of being in the imperial box by sunrise (*Life of Claudius*, 34) to watch the slaughter – a far cry from the sensitive, humane character portrayed by Robert Graves in *I, Claudius*.

As with football supporters today, rivalry spilled over into violence. Tacitus described how the people of Nuceria and Pompeii, neighbouring towns in Campania, came to blows in a riot that left many wounded or dead:

Oppidana lascivia in vicem incessentes probra, dein saxa, postremo ferrum sumpsere.

They were hurling insults at each other typical of small-town rivals; then they threw stones and in the end they drew swords.

Tacitus, *Annals,* 14.17. 4–5

A fresco in Pompeii depicts this riot – the Pompeians came out on top. After the riot, the senate made a decision Emperor Nero was reluctant to take and voted for a ten-year moratorium on gladiatorial events at Pompeii.

Eventually, the great, awful, bloody spectacles of imperial Rome went into decline. On the first day of October, 326 AD Emperor Constantine effectively cut off the main avenue of recruitment for the gladiatorial schools by this simple, cruel decree.

Damnationem ad bestias in laborem ad metalla commutari decretum est

It is decreed that condemnation to the beasts be changed to forced labour in the mines.

Cod. Theodos. 15.12.1

Constantine's conversion to Christianity caused the gladiatorial shows, the bloody *spectacula* of the arena so loved by the mob, to wither on the vine. 80 years later, an edict by the Emperor Honorius finally put an end to all gladiatorial combats in the West.

First, mime had replaced true theatre. Then Christianity ended the murderous entertainment of the amphitheatre.

'For my next slaying, I'll need a volunteer from the audience'

'Before we start, why don't we go round and each say a little something about ourselves?'

9

Plebs and Patricians – the Roman Class System

The Pope is a pleb. We don't say this out of any anti-Catholicism. It's just that the Pope, like all Catholics, belongs to the **plebs sancta – the holy people** – as they are referred to in the Latin Mass.

That Catholic definition is one of the few surviving modern uses that preserve the uncritical sense of the original word, before it was borrowed for snobbish insults. Incidentally, in Latin, the word is *plebs* in the singular, and *plebes* in the plural, while those drawn from the plebs class were called *plebeianus*, or plebeian.

By classical standards, the MP Andrew Mitchell's use of 'pleb' to a policeman in Downing Street in 2012 was incorrect, as well as disgusting. In the ancient world, not only was the policeman at the gates of Downing Street a pleb but so is Mitchell himself, as are his fellow MPs and most of the House of Lords. Perhaps only a few dukes and the Queen and her immediate family aren't plebs – although they're far too grand to use such a horribly *de haut en bas* term.

In Rome, the plebeians were really the squeezed middle: the free, land-owning Romans, with vast numbers of slaves beneath them, and the patricians a tiny, elite cadre above. There wasn't much social mobility, either; plebeian and patrician status was inherited from generation to generation. The equites (cavalrymen or knights) were the second of the property-based classes below the senatorial class.

Pretty much every Roman citizen was a pleb, even very grand ones like Pompey and Cicero; not that that stopped a sort of self-hating snobbery emerging among some plebeians. Cicero may have been a pleb but still he talked about the **sordida plebs – the disgusting poor** – in a first-century BC version of Andrew Mitchell's self-hating rant.

The word's origins are hard to nail down, but *plebs* was certainly used in the fifth-century BC Roman Republic. That there was no emperor around then didn't stop there being rigid class divisions; you only have to go to America or France today to see you don't need a monarch to produce endemic snobbery.

Still, modern snobbery has nothing on the Roman version. Our class system may be deeply rooted, but you don't get earls controlling the strings of power in one tiny political party, with massed ranks of commoners in the opposition. That's essentially what happened during the so-called Struggle of the Orders in Rome in the fourth and fifth centuries BC, when the patricians did all they could to keep the plebs from political power. Plebeians couldn't be priests or magistrates, nor could they marry into the patrician class.

But gradually the plebs fought back, getting their hands on all the major offices of state after decades of protest – at one point, they carried out the first ever sit-down strike. As early as the fifth century BC, they had their own political representatives, the Tribunes of the People. The law against intermarriage with patricians was overturned and, in 367 BC, they got access to the top job in the Roman Republic – the consulship.

You can compare the decline of Roman patricians to that of our own hereditary peers – once an extremely strong body, with automatic entitlement to political power, now reduced to their titles and a few honorary offices (apart from that rump left in the House of Lords).

By the second century BC, the patricians still called themselves that, but there was nothing they could do that the plebeians couldn't, a few hereditary priesthoods apart – not unlike those hereditary roles carried out by the Marquess of Cholmondeley and the Duke of Norfolk at British coronations.

Still, just because we've largely eradicated new hereditary peerages, and got rid of most hereditary aristocratic power, that doesn't mean the old class divisions don't go on humming away, as they did in ancient Rome. A viscount is still a viscount; and the divisions between patricians and plebeians remained throughout ancient Roman history, even after practically all the legal differences had long been removed.

Outward signs of those class divisions were treasured in the later years of imperial Rome, particularly when it came to dress: only the imperial family could wear the purple gown, dyed with expensive Tyrian purple dye, produced by crushing thousands of sea snails.

Those divisions had been worn so deeply into Roman life and language that they had their effect on this old imperial backwater long after the legionaries fled Britain in 410 AD.

The term pleb retained semi-official status in Britain right into the twentieth century. At Westminster School – Nick Clegg's alma mater – the sons of tradesmen were still called plebs as late as 1902, to distinguish them from the offspring of the nobility and gentry. In America, first years at military academies were still called plebes – good, correct Latin there – into the last century.

Through the twentieth century, it was employed as derogatory slang. James Joyce and H. G. Wells both used the word pleb in that way. 'Mrs Rode's quite decent in a plebby sort of way: doyleys and china birds,' says a character in John Le Carré's 1962 novel, *A Murder of Quality*.

But these were the last gasps for pleb as an official, or unofficial, term. By the 1970s, it had all but died out – except among chief whips and popes.

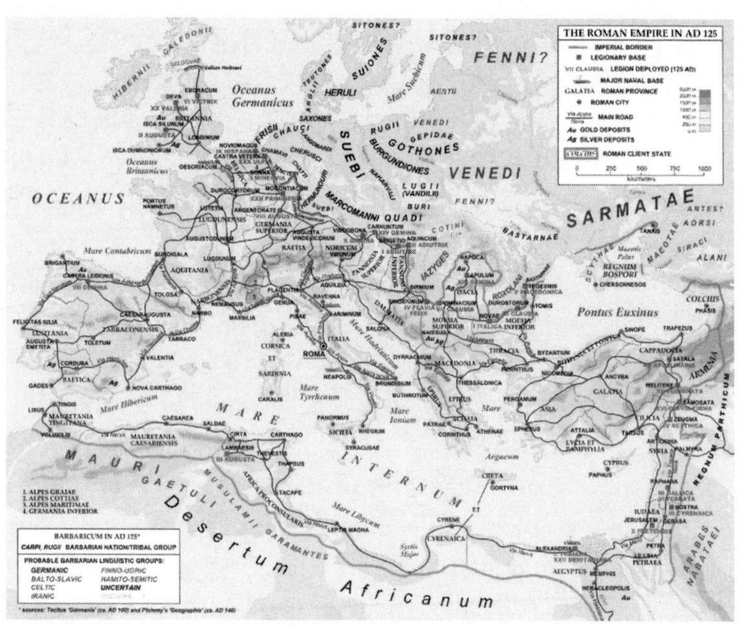

The Roman Empire in 125 AD.

10

Empire and Emperors

If any man can claim responsibility for bringing the Republic to an end and instituting the imperial period of Roman history, it is Gaius Julius Caesar (100–44 BC).

Julius Caesar refused to become emperor himself. But he adopted his great-nephew Octavian, the future Emperor Augustus, as his heir, precipitating the last phase of civil war.

Caesar did indeed 'bestride the world like a colossus', as Shakespeare's Cassius says of him. His surname was adopted, not only by all future emperors of Rome but also by more modern rulers like the tsars of Russia and the German Kaiser. Napoleon in particular liked to be portrayed as a French Caesar.

On his assassination on the Ides of March, 44 BC, Caesar also provided the most famous of all Latin quotations – and the title of this book.

Et tu, Brute?

You too, Brutus?

Suetonius, *Lives of the Caesars*, 82

In fact, Caesar and the Roman emperors spoke Greek. Julius Caesar's last words to Brutus weren't '*Et tu, Brute*', but '*Kai su, teknon*' – Greek for 'You, too, my child?'

How funny that the real, more moving, Greek words have been forgotten and the fake news – the Latin words – live on in infamy. Greek remained the first language of Roman leaders for over 350 years after Caesar's assassination.

ROMAN TIME

We are still living on Roman time.

The origins of the names of our months go back, according to legend, to a calendar set up by Romulus, the mythical founder of Rome, in the eighth century BC.

Romulus's calendar had ten months: Martius, Aprilis, Maius, Iunius, Quintilis, Sextilis, September, October, November and December. You'll see that those last six months literally mean 'the fifth', 'the sixth', etc. And that we still use September, October, November and December, even though they are no longer the seventh, eighth, ninth and tenth month of the year.

We owe the 12 months of the year – again according to legend – to Numa Pompilius, the second king of Rome after Romulus. He added in **Ianuarius** and **Februarius** – our **January** and **February**. They were originally added to the end of the year – so September, October, November and December still rang true as the seventh, eighth, ninth and tenth months.

It was Julius Caesar who messed it all up, by making January the start of the year, as it is now. And so, suddenly, December – once the tenth month – became the twelfth month.

In 44 BC, Mark Antony declared that Caesar should bequeath his name to Quintilis – what had been the fifth month, but was now the seventh month, Iulius, or July. And, in 8 BC, it was ruled that what had been the sixth month, Sextilis, and was now the eighth month, should be named after Julius Caesar's successor, Augustus. August was born.

Julius Caesar was also responsible for the most famous date in Roman history, the Ides of March – 15 March – in 44 BC, the day he was assassinated.

All Roman months had three principal days, around which the calendar revolved: the Kalends, or the first day of the month; the Ides, the thirteenth day of the month, except in March, May, July and October, when it was the fifteenth day; and the Nones, which was eight days before the Ides.

Any day immediately before the Kalends, Nones or Ides was called 'Pridie'. So *Prid. Non. Mart.*, as it was abbreviated, is 6 March. All other days were worked out by counting back from one of those three principal days.

Bear in mind that the principal day itself is counted in counting backwards. So, *III Id. Mart.* is the third day back from the Ides of March – i.e. 13 March, counting 15 March as the first day.

As well as speaking Greek, Roman emperors – and the Roman people – felt a cultural cringe towards Greek civilization. As Horace wrote of the Roman victors over Greece,

Graecia capta ferum victorem cepit et artis intulit agresti Latio.

Conquered Greece took her rough conqueror prisoner and introduced the arts to rustic Latium.

Epistles, 2.1.156–7

The 'Latio' in the Horace line above is Latium, which gave its name to modern Lazio, the region around Rome.

Latium occupied what is now the southern half of modern Lazio. It is in Latium, too, that the tribe of the Latins emerged. They first started speaking archaic Latin there in around 600 BC. As they conquered neighbouring territories, so Latin began to eclipse a host of rival Italic languages in what is now Italy: Etruscan, Oscan, Umbrian, Faliscan, Messapian and Venetic among them – what wonderful names! Until the third century BC, Latin was just one of these Italic languages, a dialect exclusive to the tiny province of Latium.

The Latin language spread by conquest in discrete stages, always after those successful military campaigns. From 100 BC to 400 AD, the number of known languages in Roman territory shrunk from 60 to 12 and, outside Africa and the Greek-dominant East, from 30 to five: Latin, Welsh, Basque, Albanian and Gaulish.

So Latin isn't a dead language. The properly dead languages are the ones toppled by Latin: who now knows any Lusitanian, Iberian or Etruscan? And by the Roman victory over those neighbouring tribes, Latin carved out its pre-eminence in the Western mind. But what Horace was saying is that although Greece was conquered by Rome, it remained the supreme artistic civilization.

Just take the classical orders of architecture. Three out of four of them are Greek, with Greek names: Doric (from the seventh century BC); Ionic (from the sixth century BC); and Corinthian (from the fifth century BC). Only one is Roman, with a Latin name: Composite (the Arch of Titus, 81 AD, in the Roman Forum, is the earliest example). And, in any case, the Composite was only a combination (**compositus** – **compound**) of two Greek orders: Ionic and Corinthian. The fifth order of architecture, the very simple Tuscan, is a Renaissance Italian invention.

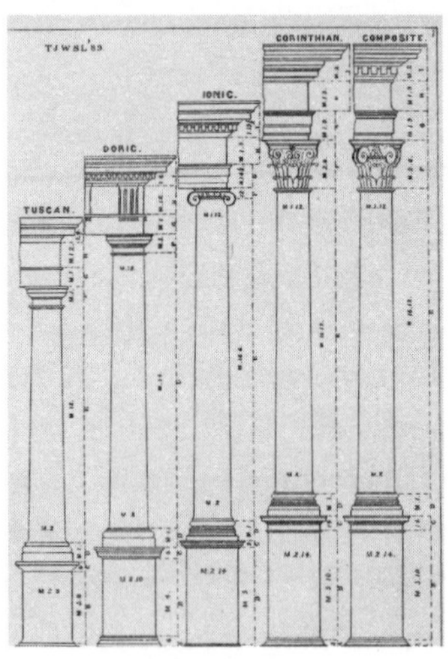

The five orders of architecture: Tuscan, Doric, Ionic, Corinthian and Composite.

The Greek influence on Latin was enormous, too. Lots of words you think are Latin are really Greek. **Nausea** (**sickness**, as in ad nauseam) comes from the Greek word *naus*, meaning 'ship'; and so it originally meant seasickness.

Greece was conquered by the Roman Republic in the Battle of Corinth in 146 BC. But, still, 200 years later, the Roman rhetorician Quintilian (35–96 AD) was, like Horace, acknowledging Greek supremacy in the arts. Of satire, one of the few art forms the Greeks didn't invent, he said:

Satura quidem tota nostra est.

Satire is indeed entirely our own.

Incidentally, it's thanks to Quintilian that we have the text message, too. In his book on speeches, Quintilian said that, after you have chosen your words, they must be woven into a fine and delicate fabric – and the Latin for **fabric** is **textum**.

Quintilian's word has clung on for 2,000 years. We still weave stories together, embroider them and try never to lose the thread of the story. Later classical writers took up 'text' to mean any short passage in a book. More recently, we started using 'text' to mean anything that was written down; and then somebody invented the SMS message, borrowing Quintilian's metaphor in the process.

Homer also remained the supreme poet to Romans, as well as Greeks. It's this line from Horace that produces our expression, 'Even Homer nods' or 'Even Homer sleeps' – i.e. even Homer makes mistakes:

Indignor quandoque bonus dormitat Homerus.

Yet I also take it amiss whenever the excellent Homer dozes off.

Horace, *Ars Poetica*, 359

As the first emperor, Augustus had his lofty position buttressed by Virgil, a genius poet and his propagandist-in-chief. In Virgil's *Aeneid*, the sovereign god Jupiter assures his troubled daughter, Venus, that her son Aeneas will triumph in the end – and lay the foundations of an **imperium**, or **empire**, on which the sun will never set.

In the *Aeneid*, Rome's task is laid out by Anchises, Aeneas's dead father, who takes him on a tour of the Underworld, pointing out the Roman heroes yet to come. He also declares to his son the purpose of the Roman empire in the future:

Romane, memento . . .
Parcere subiectis et debellare superbos.

Remember, Roman, to spare those who've submitted and subdue the arrogant.

Aeneid, 6.847

It's also in Book 6 in the Underworld that Virgil describes the dead yearning to be ferried across the River Acheron:

Tendebantque manus ripae ulterioris amore.

They reached out their hands in longing for the further shore.

Aeneid, 6.313

This line is often used to sum up a general feeling of longing. In the same way, this Aeneid line sums up the general sadness of life, as Aeneas weeps at a picture of the Trojan War in a Carthaginian temple:

Sunt lacrimae rerum et mentem mortalia tangunt.

Tears are shed for things even here and mortal things touch the heart.

Aeneid, 1.462

Seamus Heaney translated the famous first three words as 'There are tears at the heart of things.'

The two mournful lines came together in 2011 at the Chilcot Inquiry into the Iraq War. In an exchange between Sir Lawrence Freedman, Professor of War Studies at King's College London, and an anonymous MI6 officer, Sir John Chilcot, chairing the inquiry, got his Latin wrong.

> Sir Lawrence Freedman: 'What were your views of the final report of Duelfer's?'
>
> SIS4: '*Sunt lacrimae rerum*, really.'
>
> Sir Lawrence Freedman: 'Would you like to elaborate?'
>
> SIS4: 'I think it says it all.'
>
> Sir Lawrence Freedman: 'All right. We will stop there.'
>
> Sir John Chilcot: '*Tendebantque manus, ulteriore amore*. Shall we break for ten minutes?'
>
> SIS4: 'Yes, that would be lovely.'

Sir John Chilcot should have said, '*Tendebantque manus ripae ulterioris amore*.' He missed out a word and used an ablative instead of a genitive.

A related, heart-rendingly concise line came from Terence (190–159 BC):

Hinc illae lacrimae.

Hence those tears.

Terence, *Andria*, 126

The line can be used of pretty much any sad moment in life.

For the Romans, *imperium* meant supreme administrative power – whether of their early kings, certain magistrates and provincial governors, the head of a household, a military command, or the power exercised by a Roman emperor and the empire itself. Virgil thinks of the rule established by his supreme patron, Augustus, extending endlessly into the future.

His ego nec metas rerum nec tempora pono: imperium sine fine dedi.

To them [the Romans] I assign no limits in space or time: I have bestowed on them empire without end.

Virgil, *Aeneid*, 1.278–9

But the problem with a hereditary leadership is that it inevitably produces rotten apples.

Omnium consensu capax imperii nisi imperasset.

Everyone agreed that he had it in him to be an emperor, if only he hadn't become one.

Tacitus, *Histories*, 1.49

So wrote Tacitus on the death of the less than brilliant Emperor Galba (3 BC–69 AD). One of Boris Johnson's teachers at Eton quoted the line about his pupil while he was at the school. Galba met a bloody end in 69 AD, having failed to pay the money he'd promised to his soldiers and having alienated Otho, his successor.

The link between emperor and the military was crucial. As early as the final century of the Republic, Roman generals had a **cohors praetoria** – a **troop of bodyguards** who ensured their personal safety. Under Augustus, legionaries then were divorced from politics and the support of individual generals. Instead they became personally attached, as professional soldiers, to the emperor, and so to the Roman State.

The **cohors praetoria** of the Republican commander became a standing force of nine cohorts (5,400 men) – the

Praetorian Guard, established in Rome and throughout the major towns of Italy. In addition, the emperor had a private bodyguard of native Germans, huge warriors who guarded him with absolute loyalty. This bodyguard became standard among Augustus's successors.

The **cohortes praetorianae** (**Praetorians**), together with their carefully chosen **praefectus** (**commander**), formed the bedrock of imperial control in the capital. The title **imperator**, used of generals before, was now used of the emperor as **commander-in-chief**, like American presidents.

The new title **princeps** (**first citizen**) was favoured by Augustus for his unique role, perhaps in memory of the position of Pericles as 'first of men' when democracy had been created in Athens just over four centuries earlier.

Writing about the so-called 'Year of the Four Emperors', 68–9 AD, Tacitus described how Nero's death without an heir finished the Julio–Claudian dynasty – the first five emperors who had all belonged to one family.

> **Evolgato imperii arcano posse principem alibi quam Romae fieri.**
>
> **The imperial secret was out: an emperor could be made elsewhere than in Rome.**
>
> Tacitus, *Histories,* 1.4

Now the empire was up for grabs, and the controlling factor was the army. In that turbulent year, 68–9 AD, four generals vied for supremacy. Galba, Otho and Vitellius all became emperor for a short time, supported by the armies of Spain, Upper Germany and Lower Germany respectively. Finally Vespasian seized power, with the support of the legions of Egypt, Judaea and Syria. He initiated the Flavian dynasty, called after him: his full name was Titus Flavius Vespasianus.

From early on, Augustus understood the need to ensure the army's loyalty through proper pay. All his successors felt the same.

They weren't so good at spotting provincial uprisings. Historians like Tacitus recognized the importance of events taking place throughout the empire and its provinces. But, as Cicero wrote, it was easy for emperors to take their eye off the ball.

Ita multa Romae geruntur ut vix ea quae fiunt in provinciis audiantur.

So many things happen in Rome that events taking place in the provinces are hardly heard of.

Cicero, *In Defence of Plancius*, 63

Governorships were chosen by the senate as rewards for men who had served Rome as consuls or praetors. But when a province was considered a potential threat to the emperor's security – such as Egypt with its major corn-supply to the capital, or Syria, which guarded the Euphrates frontier – the emperor himself chose the governor.

At the end of Augustus's reign in 14 AD, the empire was secured by 25 legions, with almost 6,000 men per legion. Their presence guaranteed the Roman peace, establishing order for trade and commerce to flourish, underpinned by the regular collection of taxes.

Augustus saw the need for a permanent army and permanent camps in townships of strategic significance. These settlements were known as **coloniae** (**colonies**). Cologne, one of the largest, takes its name from the word.

There was a frontier system with **limites** (**boundary lines** – thus our word 'limits'). These usually aligned with natural features, like the Rhine, or buffer states ruled by friendly kings.

The loyalty of these client kings was often ensured by having their sons educated at Rome under the emperor's protection. These states were increasingly annexed by later emperors.

The constant thorn in Rome's side was the Parthian Empire in the east. The frontier was the formidable Syrian desert, as much as the River Euphrates. The Parthian Empire comprised a feudal aristocracy, serving the king as mounted archers of deadly skill, wheeling round at the last minute to take out the pursuing enemy with their 'Parthian shot'. Chinese silk – much appreciated by Roman ladies – was taxed en route to Rome by the Parthians.

By agreement, relations between Rome and Parthia were mainly diplomatic until 113 AD. That's when Emperor Trajan declared war on Parthia, eventually winning a victory at great cost to the Romans in terms of life and resources.

Trajan's Column, still standing in the Roman forum, records Trajan's earlier Dacian campaign north of the Danube, which won a triumph for him back in Rome. The best surviving record of a Roman army on the march, it reveals the Romans' technical ability as engineers, as well as their ability as soldiers. No army of comparable efficiency was seen before Cromwell's New Model Army in seventeenth-century England.

In 98 AD, Tacitus wrote the biography of his father-in-law, Agricola, Governor of Britannia from 77 to 85 AD. In it, he imagines a Scottish chieftain, Calgacus, haranguing his army before the final battle with the Roman invaders; the Battle of Mons Graupius in northern Scotland in 83 or 84 AD.

Auferre, trucidare, rapere falsis nominibus imperium, atque ubi solitudinem faciunt, pacem appellant.

They falsely give the name of empire to plunder, butchery and pillage, and where they make a desert, they call it peace.

Tacitus, *Agricola*, 30

This negative view of Roman imperial rule is quoted by other classical authors. It's the reverse of Augustan propaganda – but it's dramatic rhetoric to lend colour to the occasion, not Tacitus's personal view.

The Romans thought the necessary precondition of peace was stable government. If this could only be achieved **vi et armis (by force of arms)**, so be it. The forces of barbarism could not be allowed to prevail, if the world was to know the blessings of civilization.

Tacitus paints a gloomy picture of the reign of Augustus's successor, Tiberius, in the years after the death of Tiberius's son, Drusus, in 23 AD.

> **Saeva iussa, continuas accusationes, fallaces amicitias, perniciem innocentium.**
>
> **Cruel orders, continuous accusations, friendships based on treachery, the ruin of innocent men.**
>
> Tacitus, *Annals*, 4.33.24–6

Tacitus's criticism of the Julio–Claudian emperors in the Annals is hardly **'without anger and bias'** (**sine ira et studio**), as he had promised (*Annals*, 1.1.15). He was echoing the discontented aristocracy of Rome. They were greatly diminished in the civil wars that led to Augustus's supremacy, and further reduced by his political reforms.

Tiberius was a fine soldier and extremely intelligent. But he was forced by Augustus to divorce his adored wife and marry the emperor's widowed daughter Julia, so that Augustus's grandsons might have a father. Tiberius became embittered.

The death of his beloved brother, also called Drusus, while campaigning on the Rhine, brought out the worst in his character. Retiring to the island of Capri, he left Sejanus, his trusted Captain of the Praetorian Guard, to administer affairs in Rome. Suetonius paints a lurid picture of sexual depravity in Tiberius's declining years. Still, today's citizens of Capri are proud of their imperial resident and dismiss these allegations as malicious gossip.

Sejanus overreached himself, which caused Tiberius to send the Senate a 'long and wordy letter'. It was read out with Sejanus present. He was expecting to be named as Tiberius's successor, having married Livilla, Tiberius's daughter-in-law. He took the precaution of having her husband poisoned first. The letter ended by denouncing Sejanus as a traitor. He was attacked outside by the mob that had recently bowed down before him. They dragged his bloody corpse down to the Tiber with hooks.

Juvenal used Sejanus as an example of how favourites of the rich and powerful often come to a grisly end.

Curramus praecipites et dum iacet in ripa, calcemus Caesaris hostem.

Let's run down to the Tiber double-quick and give the emperor's enemy a good kicking, while he's lying dead on the bank there.

Juvenal, *Satires*, 10.85–6

Tiberius immediately ordered wholesale executions of Sejanus's family and friends. Juvenal's use of **hostem** here (**public enemy**) emphasizes that Sejanus had become an enemy of Rome itself, now equated with the emperor.

Delatores (**political informers**) flourished in this heightened climate of fear. They enriched themselves by bringing false charges against individuals, receiving part of their confiscated estate as a reward for the 'loyalty' they had shown the increasingly paranoid emperor.

The next emperor, Gaius, was the son of Germanicus, nephew of Tiberius. As his father was a military hero loved by the troops, the little boy would appear regularly in a soldier's uniform, wearing **caligae** (**soldier's boots**). Hence his nickname 'Caligula'.

> **Gaius, quem militari vocabulo Caligulam vocabant, quia plerumque eo tegmine pedum tegebatur.**
>
> **Gaius, whom they used to call 'Little Boot' in a military term, because for the most part this was the footwear he used to wear.**
>
> Tacitus, *Annals*, 1.41

After an auspicious start to his reign, Caligula had a severe illness. He emerged from it a monster of cruelty – 'No longer a prince,' Suetonius wrote, 'but a monstrosity' (*The Twelve Caesars*, 'Caligula', 9).

Declaring himself divine, Caligula had the heads of famous statues of gods in Rome replaced by his own. To pay for his extravagances, he exhausted the treasury bequeathed by Tiberius in less than a year, imposing heavy taxes on the people and giving full rein to those **delatores** (**informers**). He often appeared in public dressed as a woman, and made his favourite horse Incitatus a consul.

Only the sacred memory of Caligula's father and their memory of the young emperor as Little Boot kept the legions loyal and prevented an early conspiracy against him from succeeding.

Suetonius says Caligula used to practise incest with each of his three sisters in turn, favouring Drusilla above the others and turning her into a goddess when she died.

His anger mounted. A passionate fan of the Greens in the chariot races, Caligula lost his temper one day when the crowd shouted for the wrong team, and screamed, 'I wish all you Romans had just a single neck!'

In the third year of his reign, he was assassinated by two officers of the Praetorian Guard as he left the theatre, after they had separated him, briefly, from his German bodyguard. Such was the general relief that many called for an end to the Caesars and the restoration of the Republic.

Early in the reign of Nero, the philosopher Seneca wrote a cruel satire on the deification of Caligula's successor, his uncle Claudius. He alluded to Claudius's pronounced limp as he entered the courts of Olympus, quoting Virgil's description of Aeneas's little son trying to match his father's long strides as they escaped from Troy (*Aeneid*, 2.724).

Claudium vidisse se dicet iter facientem *non passibus aequis*.

He will say that he saw Claudius, making his way 'with his unequal steps'.

Seneca, *The Pumpkinification of Claudius*, 1.2

Claudius, who suffered from a kind of paralysis from early childhood, cut a poor figure beside his handsome brother Germanicus. The adjective **claudus (lame/limping)** was uncomfortably close to his name.

Addicted to gambling, the scholarly Claudius wrote histories of the Etruscans and Carthaginians, researching diligently in the Palatine Library. Robert Graves portrayed him as a clever, moral man in *I, Claudius* (1934) and *Claudius the God* (1935), dramatized for TV in 1976 by Jack Pulman, with Derek Jacobi as the emperor. Derek Jacobi's Claudius is a kinder picture than the one left by contemporary historians.

Claudius was no fool and, despite the Senate's hostility towards him, he always treated it with the utmost respect, unlike his predecessor. He removed the danger of famine in Italy by special measures, undertook important public works and improved the harbour at Ostia, where he built a fine lighthouse to help sailors.

His humane law for the protection of sick slaves outlawed the killing of slaves and gave them their freedom, if they survived their illness after being exposed in the temple of the healing god Aesculapius on Tiber Island.

His management of the provinces was good. And he extended the franchise, increasing the number of Roman citizens under Augustus by two million. In the racial hotbed of Alexandria, he was, for the time, relatively unbiased, neither giving citizenship to the Jews nor tolerating their persecution by the Greek populace. Claudius recognized the importance of securing Britain as part of the Roman Empire, and oversaw its conquest by Aulus Plautius in 43 AD, almost a century after Julius Caesar reconnoitred the island in 55 and 54 BC.

Claudius's pernicious wives dominated him. Beautiful, corrupt Messalina married her lover and attempted a coup while Claudius was away from the capital. Agrippina was determined at all costs to have the dissolute Nero, her son by an earlier husband, inherit the throne.

In 50 AD, Claudius had been persuaded to adopt Agrippina's son, then Lucius Domitius Ahenobarbus, into the Claudian family, under the name of Nero. At the same time, she was honoured with the title of Augusta, or imperial consort (*Annals*, 12.22–4).

So Agrippina enjoyed the same title as her great-grandmother, Livia. She persuaded Claudius to adopt Nero ahead of his own son, Britannicus, and arranged for Nero to marry Claudius's daughter Octavia in 53 AD, when he was 15. Agrippina was the first imperial wife to appear on coinage – a sign of her immense power at court.

Within two years, Britannicus was dead, almost certainly poisoned on Nero's orders. Tacitus describes how the teenager's sudden inability to breathe was explained to the shocked dinner guests by Nero as 'something that often happened to epileptics, a condition Britannicus had suffered from since infancy'.

Even Nero's mother, Agrippina, Tacitus said, looked at her son in horror – she knew as little as Britannicus's young sister of his deadly intentions (*Annals*, 13. 16.27–30).

Soon it was Claudius's turn. He died on 13 October, 54 AD, aged 64, apparently poisoned while eating a dish of mushrooms, his favourite food. The culprit is thought to have been Agrippina. She kept her husband's death a secret until all arrangements had been made to safeguard her son's succession. She had beaten the odds in securing the imperial succession for a son by another husband, while ending her aged husband's days by poisoning him.

Agrippina and Nero made for a formidable pair – and a fatally flawed one. Nero committed matricide because he found his mother increasingly **intolerable (praegravem)**. Tacitus described the death of Agrippina, killed on the orders of her son Nero. As she died, she demanded punishment for the part of her body which had housed such a monster.

Iam in mortem centurioni ferrum destringenti protendens uterum 'ventrem feri' exclamavit multisque vulneribus confecta est.

Now, as the centurion was drawing his sword to kill her, she cried out to him, 'Strike here!', pointing to her womb, and was despatched with many wounds.

Tacitus, *Annals*, 14.8.31–3

Still, Agrippina realized, even as she was dying at her son's hands, that authority was everything:

'Occidat dum imperet.'

'Let him kill me, so long as he rules.'

Agrippina's dying words about Nero, according to Tacitus

Tacitus showed patrician disdain for Nero's enthusiasm for acting on stage and driving chariots. Nero's tutor, the philosopher Seneca, made little impact on his wilful behaviour. Nero unfairly blamed the catastrophic fire in Rome of 64 AD on the Christians, whom he then persecuted with great savagery as religious maniacs. The apostles Peter and Paul were among his victims. For the legend that Nero fiddled while Rome burned, see **supra** (**above**).

Soon after the fire, Nero's famous **Domus Aurea** (**Golden House**), a pleasure palace on an extravagant scale, was built, with a huge statue (colossus) of him as sun god in the forecourt. As we have seen, the Colosseum, later built in the grounds of the Domus Aurea, was named after this massive sculpture. When Nero's sumptuously decorated palace was excavated in the Renaissance, to reveal its wall-paintings and ceilings, painters and architects came from all over Italy to admire and copy them.

Nero's subjects grew increasingly alienated by his outrageous behaviour. When the armies of the Rhine provinces revolted, he took his own life, with the help of a former slave. His last words before committing suicide were

'Qualis artifex pereo.'

'What an artist the world has lost in me!'

Suetonius, *Lives of the Caesars*, 49

When Tacitus described the conquest of Britain under Claudius in 43 AD, he gave great credit to the future Emperor Vespasian, then a legionary commander.

Domitae gentes, capti reges et monstratus fatis Vespasianus.

The tribes were subdued, their kings taken prisoner – and the finger of fate pointed to Vespasian.

Tacitus, *Agricola*, 13.2

Emerging as the victor from the civil wars of 68–9 AD, Vespasian was competent and shrewd – a paragon of virtue compared with the last four Julio–Claudian emperors. Much was hoped for of his new Flavian dynasty after ten years of his excellent administration restored peace and solvency to Rome. Vespasian took the important step of filling vacancies in the senate with hard-headed provincial Italians like himself. He died in his bed, sparking popular regret at his passing – an emperor without enemies.

It was Vespasian who, in around 70 AD, imposed a **urine tax** (**vectigal urinae**) on the distribution of urine from Rome's public urinals. The urine was bought for tanning and by launderers; Vespasian taxed the proceeds.

According to Suetonius, Vespasian's son Titus thought the tax was disgusting. So Vespasian brandished a gold coin and asked **whether Titus was offended by the coin's smell** (**sciscitans num odore offenderetur**). When Titus said 'No,' Vespasian said, **'But it comes from urine'** (**Atqui ex lotio est**).

This incident spawned the expression **'Pecunia non olet'** – **'Money doesn't smell.'** In other words, money's power can be separated from its means of production. As a result, Vespasian inspired the names of urinals in Italy (*vespasiano*) and France (*vespasienne*).

In 69 AD, Vespasian marched on Rome to secure the throne. It was left to his older son Titus to complete his work in bringing the troublesome province of Judaea once more under Roman control.

Caesar Titus delectus patre perdomandae Iudaeae.

Titus Caesar was chosen by his father to complete the subjugation of Judaea.

Tacitus, *Histories*, 5.1

A year later, Titus sacked the capital city of Jerusalem, crucifying survivors in hundreds on the surrounding hillsides, according to Josephus, a Romanized Jew who wrote a history of the Jewish War. The vast Jewish temple was ransacked.

Among the spoils taken off to Rome was the great, seven-branched candlestick or Menorah, installed by Solomon – of great sanctity to the Jews. The Arch of Titus, overlooking the Roman Forum, celebrates Titus's triumph. The interior of the arch shows the Menorah being paraded through the streets of Rome.

Titus's passionate affair with the Judaean princess Berenice was celebrated in Handel's opera *Berenice* (1737). The affair ended unhappily when Titus was forced by his father to send her back to her homeland after four happy years with her in Rome.

Generous to a fault, Titus repaired the financial destruction caused by the eruption of Vesuvius in 79 AD and the plague and fire that struck Rome in the following year. He completed the building of the Colosseum, and in his and his father's honour it was called the Flavian Amphitheatre. He also built the great Baths of Titus in Rome by the Esquiline Hill.

Suetonius described the narcissism of Titus's successor, his younger brother Domitian.

Mensem Octobrem Domitianum transnominavit.

He caused the name of the month of October to be changed to Domitian.

Suetonius, *Domitian*, 13.3

Domitian later made the people of Rome call him **dominus et deus – Lord and God**. Like Tiberius, he came to the throne an embittered man, intent on exercising his powers to the full. He made no pretence of respecting the Senate. Within eight years, he brought back all the horrors of treason trials, instigated by unscrupulous informers.

Tacitus portrayed Domitian as a tyrant. The emperor recalled Agricola, the historian's father-in-law, from his successful governorship of Britain, purely because he envied his standing with the Roman people.

Domitian also hypocritically condemned the Chief Vestal Virgin, whose role required absolute chastity, to be buried alive for 'immoral behaviour'.

Despite Domitian's rising unpopularity, his murder in 96 AD, as part of a conspiracy supported by his wife Domitia, was not well-received by the Praetorian Guard and the army in the provinces. They remembered that he had taken the field in person against the savage Sarmatians (in modern Iran) in 92 AD.

Still, it was only on Domitian's death that the Empire steadied itself again. 'If a man were called upon to fix that period in the history of the world during which the condition of the human race was most happy and prosperous,' Edward Gibbon wrote, 'he would, without hesitation, name that which elapsed from the death of Domitian to the accession of Commodus.'

A copy of London's earliest inscribed monument, 1st Century AD, Tower Hill. Julia Pacata put it up to her husband, procurator (or financial officer) of Britain. It means, **"To the spirits of the departed (and) of Gaius Julius Alpinus Classicianus, son of Gaius, of the Fabian voting-tribe, … procurator of the province of Britain; Julia Pacata I[ndiana], daughter of Indus, his wife, had this built."**

11

The Divine Family – Religion and the Gods

Primus in orbe deos fecit timor.

Fear first created gods in the world.

Petronius, *Poems*, 3.1

Homer set the pattern for Roman views of the gods. In Virgil's description, the supreme god, Jupiter, behaves like Zeus does in *The Iliad*. Jupiter convenes an assembly of the other gods who lived on Mount Olympus, from where they surveyed the world of humans below.

Panditur interea domus omnipotentis Olympi conciliumque vocat divum pater atque hominum rex sideream in sedem.

Then the house of all-powerful Olympus was opened wide, and the father of the gods and king of men summoned a council into his starry seat.

Virgil, *Aeneid*, 10.1–3

The language echoed the words used for calling a meeting of the Roman Senate. It cast Jupiter as the presiding magistrate, normally a consul. Virgil's phrase 'father of the gods' also reflected the traditional image of a large family of gods and goddesses under the paternal authority of Jupiter. Homer's gods had all the passions of the human race but, unlike the struggling mortals, enjoyed unending lives of pleasure and ease. Like the Roman gods, they had the final say over human lives down below, whatever our vain attempts at free will:

Dis aliter visum.

The Gods thought otherwise.

Virgil, *Aeneid*, 2.428

And there wasn't much we poor mortals could do to change their minds:

Desine fata deum flecti sperare precando.

Stop thinking the gods' decrees can be changed by praying.

Virgil, *Aeneid*, 6.376

Despite those depressing words by Virgil, Romans thought they could temper the gods' anger through **religio** – **religious observance**. They also thought the gods particularly favoured the Romans. In *The Aeneid*, Jupiter sanctioned the Roman mission of conquest and government, begun by their Trojan ancestor Aeneas. Jupiter set 'no limits of time or space' for the Roman Empire (*Aeneid*, 1. 278).

The Romans did not suffer from the burden of original sin that required them to ask perpetual forgiveness from a morally perfect deity. Instead, life should be lived to the full before the sun's brightness was lost for ever and they became, in Horace's phrase, **pulvis et umbra** (**dust and ashes**) – *Odes*, 4.7.16.

In remote parts, Romans still worshipped the old pagan gods. They were briefly officially reinstituted by the Emperor Julian (331–363 AD), known as the Apostate for rejecting Christianity. Their remoteness led to their name as **pagani** or **pagans,** from **pagus**, Latin for a **village**. The term was disrespectful, like the modern use of Luddites.

If Roman religion wasn't actively 'moral' like Christianity, it wasn't unconnected with morality, either. The Romans believed they were protected by the gods. Their temple rules and religious rites encouraged people to behave morally. Cicero explicitly stated that the purity required for those who approached the gods should transcend mere ritual and inform the **animus** (**spirit**) of the worshipper (*On the Laws*, 2.18–25).

In Rome, Jupiter was worshipped in a magnificent temple on the Capitoline Hill to 'Jupiter Greatest and Best'. The smaller temple of **Iuppiter Tonans (Jupiter the Thunderer**) was built of solid marble. Its cult statue was a masterpiece by the Greek sculptor Leochares (fourth century BC).

The oak was sacred to Jupiter. As the ruler of the skies, he brandished the **lightning bolt (fulmen** – as in fulminate) and the **thunderclap (tonitrus** – as in 'astonish') – the terrifying expression of his anger.

Juno

The epic poet Ennius described Jupiter's wife, Juno, in reverential terms.

> **Respondit Iuno Saturnia, sancta dearum.**
>
> **Juno, Saturn's child, holy among goddesses, replied.**
>
> Ennius, *Annals*, 64

Juno's father, Saturn, the Kronos of Greek myth, was a cannibalistic ogre. Juno too was given to anger – her portrayal in *The Aeneid* is reminiscent of the Wicked Queen's. When she is called **sancta (holy)**, her holiness isn't like the holiness of the Virgin Mary. It is testimony to her awful power in heaven and earth as the consort of Jupiter.

As the greatest goddess, she was associated with childbirth and marriage and venerated by Roman women. She was worshipped, along with Jupiter, in his great Capitoline temple and had her own splendid temple, to **Iuno Regina (Queen Juno)**, on the Aventine Hill.

In her guardianship of the sanctity of marriage, Juno was regarded as the model for all Roman matrons and inspired the character of Wotan's wife in Wagner's *Ring*. Like her long-suffering Greek equivalent Hera, Juno had to put up with her almighty husband's many affairs with mortal women.

Apollo, God of the Sun

Apollo, the most handsome god, was the son of Jupiter and Latona, a beautiful mortal. He was associated with prophecy, archery, medicine and the sun, as well as music and poetry.

His first appearance in literature is early in Homer's *Iliad*, when he rains arrows of pestilence down on the Greek camp for nine days to punish their king who had dishonoured his priest Calchas.

Apollo is the only Roman god among the Olympians who retains his Greek name. It derives from the Greek verb *apollumi*, 'to destroy'.

Apollo's role as Homer's Lord of the Silver Bow, dealing in death, was seized on by the Augustan propagandists. They wanted to celebrate the Battle of Actium in 31 BC – the sea engagement that decided the outcome of the civil war between Octavian, the future Emperor Augustus, and his rival, Mark Antony, lover of Cleopatra. The Egyptian fleet was apparently routed by Apollo's arrows in support of the future master of the world.

And so Octavian adopted Apollo as his patron deity, creating a magnificent complex on the Palatine Hill. It consisted of his own house and the closely connected Temple of Apollo with its fine porticoes and library.

Rome's founder and first king, Romulus, once lived on this hill. A replica of his thatched hut, the **casa Romuli (house of Romulus**), was built in front of this complex. The symbolism was clear: Romulus was Rome's first founder, and Octavian/Augustus was its second, destined to join the gods, too. After the destruction of the civil wars, he had created the new Rome and a new golden age.

Apollo's oracle at Delphi was consulted by people from all over the Graeco–Roman world. And, as the sun god (Phoebus), Apollo drove his team of horses over the sky, bringing light to the world, as he returned each day – 'putting the stars to flight', in Horace's phrase (*Odes*, 3.21.24).

The laurel was sacred to Apollo – so laurel wreaths were worn by poets from antiquity to Dante. From Homer onwards, poets claimed to be conduits for the Muses – the goddesses who, together with Apollo, presided over the arts, especially poetic composition.

The Nine Muses, like Apollo, were originally Greek: Clio (history); Polyhymnia (music); Urania (astronomy); Euterpe (harmony); Erato (lyric and love poetry); Terpsichore (dancing); Thalia (comedy); Melpomene (tragedy); and Calliope (epic poetry).

The love poet, Propertius, was an exception. He gave the credit for his poetry neither to Calliope, the muse of poetry, nor Apollo, god of music and poetry, but to the girl he loved, Cynthia.

Non haec Calliope, non haec mihi cantat Apollo:
ingenium nobis ipsa puella facit.

Neither Calliope nor Apollo sang these verses to me:
my girl herself was my source of inspiration.

Propertius, *Elegies*, 2.1.3–4

Diana, Goddess of the Hunt

Diana, Apollo's twin sister, was associated with hunting, virginity and the moon.

Moonless nights were explained by the times that Diana, appearing as the Moon, slipped away to visit a beautiful youth, Endymion, in his cave on Mount Latmos. There he slept for ever, illuminated by her chaste, loving beams.

As heavenly brother and sister, Apollo and Diana were held up in Augustan art and poetry as patrons of peace and plenty. They were the visible manifestations of the world order introduced by the beneficent Augustus – **the pax Romana** (**Roman peace**).

More sinisterly, Diana was worshipped as **Trivia**, **goddess of the crossways**, where unsavoury people and practices abounded. *Trivia* is the plural of *trivium* – the place where three roads meet. *Trivia* came to mean a public or open place – and so, by extension, **trivialis** came to mean **public** or **commonplace** and thus trivial.

The poet Lucretius, in his attack on the 'irrational religiosity' of his fellow Romans, recalled the story of the virgin Iphigeneia. She was sacrificed by her father, Agamemnon, at **Triviai virginis aram – the altar of the Maiden of the Crossways** *(On the Nature of Things,* 1. 84*)*. A priest had assured Agamemnon only a virgin's blood would appease the virgin goddess and grant a fair wind to his becalmed fleet desperate to get to Troy to fight the Trojan War. The poet's comment has been much anthologized:

> **Tantum religio potuit suadere malorum.**
>
> **Such are the depths of wickedness men can plumb when driven by religious belief.**

Lucretius, *De Rerum Natura,* 1.101

Diana is predominantly represented in art as a huntress. Thus Lord Spencer's address at Princess Diana's funeral in 1997:

> 'It is a point to remember that of all the ironies about Diana, perhaps the greatest was this – a girl given the name of the ancient goddess of hunting was, in the end, the most hunted person of the modern age.'

Like her divine twin, Diana showed the gods' capacity for exacting a terrible revenge if slighted. Actaeon the young huntsman was changed into a stag and torn apart by his own hounds for inadvertently seeing the goddess in a forest glade, naked at her bath. Titian was particularly keen on painting the story.

Ovid advised young men in Rome, who were in a relationship they wanted to end, to try the pleasures of hunting, far away from their mistress, in a forest glade untouched by the sun's rays. 'Often Venus has beaten a retreat,' Ovid wrote, 'shamefully vanquished by the sister of Phoebus [Apollo, as god of the sun]' (*Cures for Love*, 199–200).

Across the Empire, Diana was one of the most popular goddesses. The historian Livy described one of the Seven Wonders of the World, the vast Temple of Diana (also known as the Temple of Artemis) at Ephesus in Asia Minor, modern Turkey.

Inclitum Dianae Ephesiae fanum.

The famed temple of Diana at Ephesus.

Livy, *History of Rome*, 1.45.2

It was at Ephesus that the apostle Paul was nearly lynched by an angry mob, only to be saved by soldiers when he shouted out that he was a Roman citizen.

Venus, Goddess of Love

Venus, goddess of love, was one of the most powerful Roman deities, for obvious reasons. She stands in for all aspects of love, as Horace implied in his Epistles.

> **Singula de nobis anni praedantur euntes eripuere iocos, Venerem, convivia, ludum.**
>
> **The passing years rob us of all pleasures, one by one; they snatch away jokes, Venus [or, in other words, love], feasts and playing.**
>
> *Epp.*, 2.2.55–6

The poet Propertius said the world was completely pleasure-free if his love life wasn't prospering.

> **Nam quis divitiis adverso gaudet Amore? Nulla mihi tristi praemia sint Venere.**
>
> **For who delights in wealth when Love frustrates him? I don't want any such rewards if Venus frowns on me.**
>
> Propertius, *Elegies*, 1.14.15–16

The goddess Venus, like her Greek equivalent, Aphrodite, presided over sexual love and generation. Her power extended over all creatures, including her divine father, Jupiter. Her name was synonymous with the act of love itself. Consequently Venus is the most powerful of the Olympians. As we saw Virgil say earlier, **Omnia vincit amor** (**Love conquers everything**).

The poet Lucretius began his great poem on the atomic nature of the world, ***De Rerum Natura*** (**On the Nature of**

Things), by addressing a prayer to Venus as the creative force of Nature, asking her to bring peace to the world.

Venus's mischievous son, Cupid, was often shown blindfolded, showing that love is blind. His flame-tipped arrows created the fire of love in men and women, mortal and divine.

In Virgil's national epic, *The Aeneid*, as in Homer's *Iliad*, Venus is the mother of Aeneas (by the Trojan Anchises). She is a counterbalance to the machinations of Juno, her malevolent stepmother.

The Augustan poets celebrated her as Venus Genetrix, ancestress of the Roman people and the **gens Iulia – the Julian family**. Its most famous members were Julius Caesar and his adopted son Octavian/Augustus.

In Rome, Venus's temple looked out on the Forum of Caesar. Its apse (the first in a Roman temple) held the cult statues of the god Mars (her divine lover), the goddess herself and **Divus Iulius** (**deified Julius**).

The Roman peace was won through military victories, as everyone accepted, and Venus was also seen as **Venus Victrix** (**Goddess of Victory**). Augustus recognized that war and victory were the precondition of the Pax Augusta – his much celebrated peace – that underpinned and justified his rule. In this capacity, the goddess was transformed from the Greek embodiment of sexual desire to the kindly mother of the Roman nation, presiding over its burgeoning empire.

But love poets preferred to dwell on Venus's erotic aspect as the essence of human sexuality. She was portrayed naked by sculptors (before her Augustan remake as a respectable matron) and as the paradigm of female beauty in all its erotic attraction. Her fourth-century BC cult statue on the peninsula of Cnidus by the Greek master Praxiteles was deliberately placed so that it could be viewed from all angles. Its erotic charge was so great that a tourist industry developed around it, to the benefit of the island's economy. The statue was said to be so realistic that a young man sexually assaulted it.

Venus was married to Vulcan, the ugly, crippled smith of the gods, in recognition of the fact that a conventional marriage was impossible for the epitome of sexual allure.

Among her many handsome lovers was the god Mars. Renaissance artists often painted the lusty war god in post-coital slumber in the goddess's lap, as she gazed out at the onlooker in quiet triumph – Botticelli's *Mars and Venus* (1483) in the National Gallery is the best example.

In *The Odyssey*, Homer told how Mars and Venus were caught *in flagrante* by Vulcan, literature's first cuckold. Vulcan cast a net he had forged over them, so that they couldn't move. He then invited his fellow deities to view the comically cruel sight.

Venus was also the word for the best throw in dicing, in which Romans of all classes participated. Four dice were thrown and when each of the four sides turned up a different number, that was a **Venerius – a Venus throw**.

Venus didn't always get such favourable press. Martial, with his reliably jaded outlook, uses her name as an alternative word for a prostitute. He wrote that a **plebeia Venus – a bog-standard prostitute** – was to be had for **gemino asse** or **two coppers** (*Epigrams*, 2.53.7).

Mars, God of War

Virgil described the gates of the Temple of Janus in Rome.

> **Sunt geminae Belli portae (sic nomine dicunt) religione sacrae et saevi formidine Martis.**
>
> **There are two gates of War (this is how they are known), sanctified by religious belief and the fear inspired by savage Mars.**
>
> Virgil, *Aeneid*, 7.607–8

When those gates were closed, Rome was at peace. They were closed in 29 BC, two years before the Senate conferred the title 'Augustus' on Octavian. The closure showed that, 'throughout the entire empire of the Roman people, on land and sea, peace had been won through victories' (*Res Gestae*, 13). The **Res Gestae Divi Augusti – the Things Done by Divine Augustus** – were the achievements listed by Augustus himself just before his death in 14 AD. Copies were carved in stone across the empire.

That description of Mars, god of war, as 'savage' recalls Homer's portrayal of the god Ares (the Greek equivalent of Mars), hated by mortals and gods alike, who delighted in indiscriminate bloodshed. When Virgil described the horror of the civil war which ravaged Italy throughout the first century BC, he referred to **Mars impius (the god of unholy strife)**, since families were often torn apart, as in seventeenth-century England during the Civil War.

All the same, Romans venerated Mars as the father of Romulus and Remus and the source of their military success. The large area on the banks of the Tiber where young men exercised and trained for war was the **Campus Martius** (**Field of Mars**).

In 42 BC, Octavian made a vow to build a temple to **Mars Ultor** (**Mars the Avenger**) to commemorate his act of revenge on Caesar's assassins at the Battle of Philippi. He fulfilled this vow after the diplomatic victory over the Parthians in 20 BC, when the Roman standards, lost to them 33 years earlier, were returned and installed in the new temple in the Forum of Augustus.

Mars also appears in the sculptures on the west side of the great **Ara Pacis Augustae** (**Altar of Augustan Peace**) on the Field of Mars (9 BC), emphasizing that peace was won by military victories.

The Romans could certainly be savage – in the relentless machine of their army or the bloodthirsty appetite of the Colosseum's crowds. In a similar way, Romulus and Remus were exposed as infants and suckled by a she-wolf – a symbol of savagery in the Italian countryside, much feared by farmers.

But, unlike many warlike nations, the Romans created a system of government and law that sought to deliver justice, using war as a means towards peace. Mars appeared alongside that wolf-nurse in the same relief on the Altar of Peace, linking the two with Rome's founding father. On an Augustan relief, Mars is shown with a cornucopia, from which the baby twins, Romulus and Remus, spring. They reach out for a trophy, commemorating the subjection of the Parthians.

Cornucopia comes from **cornu** (**horn**) and **copia** (**plenty**) – horn of plenty. In other words, peace and prosperity grow out of war and strife.

Minerva, Goddess of Wisdom

Minerva was identified with the goddess Athena, the Greek goddess of handicrafts, wisdom, learning and the arts.

The comic poet Terence wrote about Minerva's miraculous birth from the head of her father, Jupiter. She sprang fully formed from his head, dressed in armour.

> **Si ex capite sis meo natus, item ut aiunt Minervam esse ex Iove.**
>
> **If you were born from my head, just as, they say, Minerva was from Jupiter.**
>
> Terence, *The Self-Tormentor*, 1036

Her unorthodox birth was reflected in her dual nature as goddess of learning and victory in war. As a result, someone of great versatility was known as **Homo omnis Minervae** (**a person with every [quality of] Minerva**) (Petronius, *Satyricon*, 43.8).

Athena was the patron goddess of Athens, the city to which she gave her name. She was credited, too, with the discovery of the olive. As goddess of wisdom, she gave her name to the Athenaeum, the cleverest club in London, historically associated with dons and bishops.

Ovid wrote about a girl named Arachne, who challenged Minerva to a weaving contest. The goddess was so angered by the excellence of the girl's tapestry that she attacked her with her shuttle. Defiantly the girl tried to escape punishment by trying to hang herself. Minerva turned her into a spider (*arachne* in Greek), condemning her and her descendants to live forever suspended in the air (Ovid, *Metamorphoses*, 6.5–145).

When the poet Martial wanted to describe the office of librarian to the emperor, he hit on the clever phrase **Palatinae cultor Minervae** (**votary of Minerva of the Palatine**). The emperor's librarian was in charge of the great library of Greek and Roman writers next to that Temple of Apollo, built by Augustus on the Palatine Hill.

Minerva was popularly associated with intelligence. Thus the widespread proverb **Sus Minervam docet – A pig teaches Minerva**: used of someone trying to instruct a person much wiser than himself.

Mercury, Messenger of the Gods

Identified with the Greek Hermes, Mercury was the messenger of the gods, equipped with winged sandals and **caduceus** (**wand**). He also guided the dead down to their final resting-place in the Underworld. Associated with luck and sleight of hand, Mercury was the patron god of money-making – and thieves. The pickpocket Autolycus in *The Winter's Tale* claims to be 'litter'd under Mercury', to whom he owes his success as a confidence trickster. The name probably derives from the plural of the Latin word for **merchandise** (**merces**).

Lyric poets were regarded as **viri Mercuriales (Mercury's men)**, the favourites of the god who invented the lyre and gave mankind the gift of music.

In the quotation below, Horace calls Mercury 'grandson of Atlas' because he was the son of Jupiter by the beautiful nymph Maia, Atlas's daughter. The 'mercurial' nature of Mercury caused scientists to use his name to describe the element that is both solid and liquid – known as quicksilver, an apt word for the god who moved with such effortless speed from heaven to earth.

Mercury was always a special god in Horace's eyes, associated with eloquence, civilization and fun. As a man who enjoyed a party and female company, Horace was devoted to Mercury as a companion of Venus – but above all as the inventor of the lyre (made from a tortoiseshell).

Horace – who flourished as the lyric poet par excellence in Augustan Rome and, after the death of Virgil, as poet laureate – felt he was under the god's protection.

Mercuri, facunde nepos Atlantis . . . te canam, magni Iovis et deorum nuntium, curvaeque lyrae parentem.

Mercury, eloquent grandson of Atlas . . . I will sing of you, messenger of mighty Jupiter and the gods, father of the curved lyre.

Horace, *Odes,* 1.10. 1 and 5–6

Horace jokingly attributed his survival at the Battle of Philippi in 42 BC to the god whisking him off the battlefield, like a Homeric hero.

That battle, in Macedonia, was between Mark Antony and Octavian, on one side, and Brutus and Cassius on the other. Brutus and Cassius led the plot to kill Caesar two years earlier on the Ides of March, 15 March, 44 BC. Cassius killed himself, but the battle was otherwise inconclusive. Horace, fighting on Brutus's side, claimed, perhaps in a self-deprecating way, that he fled the battlefield without his shield.

Pluto, God of the Underworld

The satirist Juvenal imagined a time in the distant past when the Homeric family of gods didn't inhabit Olympus or the Underworld, and didn't yet attract worshippers to temples.

Nondum aliquis sortitus triste profundi imperium, aut Sicula torvus cum coniuge Pluton.

No monarch had yet allotted to him the gloomy realms below; no grim Pluto was there, with his Sicilian wife.

Juvenal, *Satires*, 13.49–50

The name Pluto smacks of black humour. It means 'the wealthy god' (as in plutocrat): his kingdom was constantly enriched by the dead.

As Jupiter's brothers, Neptune and Pluto were senior gods. The sea and the underworld were assigned to each of them respectively. Pluto was thought to be pitiless and formidable, dwelling in a grim palace among the shadows.

The 'Sicilian wife' Juvenal mentions is Proserpina (Persephone to the Greeks), who was carried off by Pluto as she picked flowers in her native Sicily. A wonderful wall painting from the tomb of Philip, father of Alexander the Great, shows the king of the underworld driving his chariot down to the underworld with the distraught girl as his prisoner. As Pluto's consort, Proserpina was worshipped as a goddess. Tacitus described how there was a temple to her near Sinope, a Greek colony in Paphlagonia in Anatolia (*Histories*, 4.84).

For Roman poets, Pluto symbolized the inexorable nature of death, and the need to grasp life's pleasures and enjoy each day to the full. Only the music of Orpheus's lyre was able to charm Pluto into letting Orpheus's dead wife, Eurydice, return with her husband to the upper world – on the condition that he didn't see her until they reached the light of day.

He looked back, 'forgetful and conquered by love'. Eurydice was swept back to her ghostly existence for ever: 'The pitiless monarch's pact was broken, and three times a crash rang out over the waters of his realm.' Eurydice held out to Orpheus her 'hands, whose strength was gone' (Virgil, *Georgics*, 4. 491–2; 498).

Pluto was equated with Dis, a Roman God of the Underworld. His name, shortened from **dives (rich)**, is also associated with wealth. One Roman woman's movingly simple epitaph was:

NVNC DATA SVM DITI.

NOW AM I GIVEN OVER TO DIS.

Corpus of Latin Inscriptions, 1.1732.7

Latin is unusually well-suited to the subject of death and epitaphs. Perhaps because the Romans were so open in confronting death, not least through addressing Pluto, they were gifted at writing about it. Or perhaps because of Latin's concision, it crams so much into so few words.

In his ***Consolatio ad Marciam*** – **Consolation for Marcia** – Seneca consoled a Roman woman who'd lost her father and son. Who couldn't be moved by these words: 'They have now been released into the free and vast spaces of eternity; no dividing seas stand between them. The path before them now is level, and they move swiftly and without obstacle in a reciprocal coexistence with the stars.' Seneca goes on to say, 'Why weep for the end of life – the whole of it deserves our tears.'

And then there's the heart-stopping simplicity of the Propertius line,

Solus ero, quoniam non licet esse tuum.

I'll be alone if I cannot be yours.

Martial wrote the most moving poem of all, for a girl who died six days before her sixth birthday, addressed to the earth on her grave: 'Be light on her because she was light on you.'

Ceres, Goddess of Agriculture

Ceres (as in cereal) was the goddess of fruits and grain and the mother of Proserpina. She was identified with the Greek goddess Demeter, and her cult on the Aventine Hill dated from the earliest days of the Republic. Like Apollo, she had her own games, the Ludi Ceriales, which lasted for a week every April.

She was much adored as a goddess. In *Copa*, Virgil's poem about an innkeeper, he writes:

Est hic munda Ceres, est Amor, est Bromius.

Here there is Ceres' pure gift, with Love and Drink.

Bromius was an alternative name for Bacchus, and Ceres here is the symbol of bread and fine food. So here was an inn combining the best kind of food, drink and love.

After the Greek destruction of Troy, the Trojan survivors, 'mothers and fathers, young and old, gathered for exile, a pitiful throng', at a mound on the outskirts of Troy 'with an ancient temple of abandoned Ceres' (Virgil, *Aeneid*, 2.713–4; 797–8). Among these wretched victims of war was Aeneas, whose wife, Creusa, died that night in the sack of Troy.

Alma Ceres (**kindly Ceres**) knew the pain of family loss, too. Ceres's daughter, Proserpina, was allowed by Pluto, God of the Underworld, to spend half of the year on earth with her mother – in those seasons, spring and summer, the trees were in leaf and crops flourished, echoing Ceres's happiness. In autumn and winter, when all was withered and bare, Ceres mourned her daughter's enforced absence, back down in the Underworld.

A favourite image was **Flava Ceres** (**fair-haired Ceres**), wearing a crown of grain ears and holding a cornucopia. She would have appeared like this in *The Tempest*, when Shakespeare has her sing her own blessing in the masque at the end of the play.

Ceres presided over the all-important supply of **corn** (**annona**) and other food to Rome under the emperors. So she often appeared in inscriptions as **Annona Augusti Ceres – Ceres, Augustus's corn-supplier.** As Jupiter's sister, she was one of the senior deities, particularly venerated by the **plebs** (**ordinary people**), whose lives depended on her bounty.

But Ceres had her downside. Ovid complained that his girlfriend lived a chaste existence during the festival of Ceres, as Roman women were required to do.

Annua venerunt Cereali tempora sacri: secubat in vacuo sola puella toro.

The time of sacred Ceres's yearly festival came round: my girl lay alone in her bed at night.

Ovid, *Amores*, 3.10.1–2

Neptune, God of the Sea

Neptune, identified with the Greek Poseidon, was the god of the sea. His temples were usually sited on promontories, like the one perched on Cape Sounion, south of Athens, where Byron scratched his name on a column. Shipwrecks were common in the ancient world – and so there were shrines in his honour across the Mediterranean.

In one Plautus comedy, a character expressed his gratitude to Neptune for letting him and his precious cargo return safely from a dangerous sea-voyage.

Salsipotenti et multipotenti Iovi fratri Neptuno gratias maxumas ago.

I offer my greatest thanks to you, Neptune, brother of Jupiter, omnipotent, salti-potent.

Plautus, *Trinummus* (A Three-Dollar Day), 820–1

Neptune was much feared as a god who was **saevomque severumque atque avidis moribus – savage and severe and greedy in his morals**, as the Plautus character goes on to tell us.

To be hated by the god of the sea – like Homer's Odysseus – was a terrible fate. Neptune could create earthquakes, raise storms or fill sails with favourable winds – making him feared on land, as well as at sea. He was also associated with the bull and the horse, which sprang originally from the earth when struck by Neptune's trident.

Such a powerful god was a propaganda gift in the civil wars of the late first century BC. Octavian (later Emperor Augustus) is represented as Neptune on a cameo from the 30s BC. Driving a chariot over the waves, he dominates an enemy who disappears into them: either Sextus Pompey or, more probably, Mark Antony, who was persuaded by Cleopatra, disastrously, to fight the decisive battle at sea.

Octavian dedicated a statue to Neptune at Actium, the site of his great victory over Mark Antony and Cleopatra in 31 BC. In fact, everyone knew that Octavian had stayed below decks, being seasick, while his admiral Agrippa won the day. But the real loser was Antony, 'a strumpet's fool', as Shakespeare called him.

On a coin issued shortly after the battle, the young Octavian was called 'Caesar, son of the god', four years before the Senate voted him the title Augustus. He poses, heroic and nude, as Neptune, with a trident in his hand and his right foot resting on a globe.

Neptune figured prominently in mosaics and reliefs, notably in a marble relief of ships at Ostia, the port of Rome, dating from around 200 AD. The god also appeared regularly in Renaissance and baroque fountains – most famously in the Trevi Fountain in Rome, immortalized in the Anita Ekberg sequence in Fellini's *La Dolce Vita* (1961). The gold salt-cellar Bernini made for Francis I, now in Vienna, shows Neptune holding his trident as he reclines and gazes at a nymph who represents Earth.

In the first simile in *The Aeneid*, Virgil compares Neptune, calming the storm that wrecked the Trojan fleet, to a great statesman bringing order to a mob through the power of his oratory and his natural authority. And then Neptune, having calmed things down, flies off in his chariot:

Sic cunctus pelagi cecidit fragor, aequora postquam
prospiciens genitor caeloque invectus aperto
flectit equos curruque volans dat lora secundo.

In the same way, all the crashing of the sea subsides, after father Neptune, gazing out over the sea, carried through the clear sky, turned his horses and gave rein to them, flying behind in his chariot.

Virgil, *Aeneid*, 1.154–6

Vulcan, God of Vulcanic Fire

Vulcan (or Volcan) was the Roman god of volcanic fire.

Volcanic eruptions were common, especially in Campania and Sicily. The most famous was the eruption of Vesuvius in 79 AD, witnessed and described by Pliny the Younger (*Letters*, 6.16).

From the late Republic onwards, however, the Romans worshipped Vulcan mainly as the averter of fires, under the title **Quietus (the Pacifier)**. He was identified with the Greek god Hephaestus, whose temple in the Athenian agora is the best preserved anywhere.

Vulcan's temples always stood outside the city, according to Vitruvius (*On Architecture*, 1.7.1), as he presided over destructive fire. His temple at the foot of the Capitol probably dates from a time when the forum lay outside the city. Vulcan, son of Jupiter and Juno, was lame after his father flung him in rage from the heights of Olympus onto the island of Lemnos, the seat of his ancient Greek cult.

Cuckolded by his wife, Venus, goddess of love, Vulcan was a figure of fun to the other gods, who mocked his awkward gait while he served them wine (Homer, *Iliad*, 1.599–600). His principal task was to forge Jupiter's thunderbolts. Horace portrays the god as a grimy blacksmith, directing the giant Cyclopes as they forge those thunderbolts, deep in the caverns below Mount Etna.

Dum gravis Cyclopum Volcanus ardens visit officinas.

While burning Vulcan visits the grim workshop of the Cyclopes.

Horace, *Odes*, 1.4.8

This scene was often painted by later artists, including Tintoretto and Velázquez.

Virgil describes Vulcan directing the Cyclopes to forge a great shield for Aeneas, just as Hephaestus had done for Achilles in *The Iliad*:

Alii ventosis follibus auras
accipiunt redduntque, alii stridentia tingunt
aera lacu. Gemit impositis incudibus antrum.
Illi inter sese multa vi bracchia tollunt
in numerum versantque tenaci forcipe massam.

Some deftly ply the windy bellows, which receive and give the roaring blasts; some plunge in cooling pond the hissing metal, while the smithy floor groans with the anvil's weight, as side by side they lift their giant arms in numbered blows and roll with gripe of tongs the ponderous bars.

Virgil, *Aeneid*, 8.449–53; John Dryden's translation

Aeneas is Venus's son by Anchises, her Trojan lover. Despite this, the adulterous goddess has no trouble in seducing her cuckolded husband, Vulcan. As a result, he's happy to make the shield for Aeneas. After they make love, Vulcan falls into a deep sleep.

Optatos dedit amplexus placidumque petivit
coniugis infusus gremio per membra soporem.

He gave her the kisses she longed for, and fell into a peaceful sleep, resting on her lap, entwined in her limbs.

Virgil, *Aeneid*, 8.405–6

In the centre of Aeneas's wondrous shield, **Vulcan Ignipotens** (**Lord of Fire**) fashioned the scene of Octavian's decisive victory at the **Battle of Actium** (**Actia bella**), over Cleopatra. Cleopatra is shown on the shield, **'amid the carnage, paling at her imminent death'**:

> **Illam inter caedes pallentem morte futura.**
>
> Virgil, *Aeneid*, 8.709–10

Virgil makes Vulcan know the future – a power not shared by Aeneas, the founder of the Roman race. He hoists the shield on his shoulders. He marvels at but doesn't understand the scenes portraying **famamque et fata nepotum – the fame and fortunes of his descendants** (Virgil, *Aeneid*, 8.731). That word **nepos – grandson** or **descendant** – is where we get 'nepotism' from, incidentally.

Bacchus, God of Wine

Bacchus was identified with the Greek Dionysus. A god of eastern origin, he was associated with orgiastic worship, revelry – and wine.

Horace associated Bacchus with poetic inspiration – Dionysus was also the god of drama. As a poet, Horace thought he had special access to Bacchus's gifts.

> **Bacchum in remotis carmina rupibus vidi docentem – credite posteri.**
>
> **I saw Bacchus among the lonely crags, teaching songs – believe me, generations to come.**
>
> Horace, *Odes*, 2.19.1–2

The god was frequently hailed as **Liber (the Freedom-Giver)** because wine rid mortals of their inhibitions and conventions, and made them forget their troubles.

Octavian's enemy Mark Antony imagined himself as 'the new Dionysus', a role supported by his legendary capacity for wine.

All the same, images of the god and his vine were successfully incorporated into Augustan art, combining with those of Apollo and his laurel, without any awkward associations with Antony. It was handy to use Bacchus as a source of nature's bounty, and therefore an integral part of the Augustan Peace – to show how the world enjoyed the benefits of a second Golden Age under Rome's second founder.

Bacchus was also a dangerous god of frightening power when angered, as several myths showed. So it was particularly important for the Romans to placate and honour him.

The most famous Renaissance portrayal of Bacchus is by Titian, who painted the young god leaping from his chariot drawn by panthers, to embrace the lovely princess Ariadne, abandoned by her faithless lover, Theseus, on the island of Naxos. The story was told by Catullus (*Poems*, 64.251–64) and set to music by Richard Strauss in his opera *Ariadne auf Naxos*.

The young Michelangelo carved Bacchus in Carrara marble for Lorenzo de' Medici and his humanist circle. He was depicted as an inebriated young man, crowned with vine leaves and grapes, his body handsome but bloated, with no trace of the nobility of the ancient gods, as he holds up an ornate wine-cup. No classical sculptor would have portrayed a god in such an unflattering way.

Oriental Gods

The Romans admitted several oriental gods into their religious practice, including the Egyptian deities Isis, Osiris and Serapis. There was also Cybele, the Anatolian **Magna Mater** (**Great Mother**), sometimes called **Mater Salutaris** (**Lady of Salvation**), mother of the gods.

When they conquered other territories, the Romans didn't impose their own gods. As part of their policy of **Romanitas**

(**Romanization**), they preferred to incorporate local deities into their own religion. Mithras was a Persian deity, and the most popular foreign god worshipped by the Romans – as in this prayer.

> **Phoebe parens .. adsis .. seu te roseum Titana vocari .. seu praestat Osirim . . . seu Persei sub rupibus antri . . . Mithram.**
>
> **Father Phoebus, come to us, whether your wish is to be called rosy Titan, Osiris or, beneath the crags over Perseus's cave, Mithras.**
>
> Statius, *Thebaid*, 1.720

Mithras worship was carried across much of Europe, mainly by the army, from the second century AD. The Romans continued with the Romanization approach when they invaded Britannia under the Emperor Claudius in 43 AD.

Another of Mithras's many shrines was on Hadrian's Wall. An inscription to him reads,

> **Invicto Mithrae Dioscoro.**
>
> **To Mithras the Invincible, Son of God.**
>
> *Corpus of Latin Inscriptions*, 1.1113

The Mithras cult was so widespread, from Asia to Africa, from the Danube to the Solway, that it could have become the universal religion of the empire rather than Christianity. It was, accordingly, targeted by the fathers of the Church, who rightly saw in it a dangerous rival.

As a huge sponge for local deities it had absorbed into Roman religious practice, the Roman Empire then exported them to expanding corners of the Empire. In the London Mithraeum, archaeologists found a head of Serapis, the Egyptian god of birth and rebirth, sporting a **modius (corn measure)**, with a hole in his skull to hold real ears of corn. In Southwark, a ceramic flagon has been found with a scratched inscription to a temple of Isis.

Empire also brought a vast influx of people from different countries. Funerary inscriptions from Corinium, Roman Cirencester, refer to a Swiss soldier from a cavalry unit in the Moselle Valley in Germany, and a Frisian from the Netherlands, who belonged to a mounted unit raised in Thrace.

It was a brilliant way of ruling by consent, rather than by the sword. Why bash up the Egyptians or the British Celts, and ban their cults? Much better to absorb those cults into your own religion, and let local chieftains jump into the *caldarium* before donning a toga and becoming quasi-Romans. Bingo! Empire on the cheap, with minimal local disruption, apart from the odd rebellion, like Boadicea's in 61 AD.

And so the Romans in Britain absorbed local British cults and British names – inscriptions show people with Roman names giving their children Gallo–British names.

At the eastern end of Hadrian's Wall, the Roman soldiers built a rectangular, stone sanctuary to a local British god, Antenociticus. His stone head, with wild, staring eyes and curly horns in his hair, survives.

At Birrens in south-west Scotland, there's a charming, monumental relief of an apparently British goddess, Brigantia, worshipped by the Brigantes in a vast area stretching from Yorkshire to Dumfries and Galloway.

Even the most famous of Roman Britain's spa resorts, Bath, was probably sacred to a British god. The Roman name for Bath was **Aquae Sulis – the Waters of Sulis**. Sulis was, it seems, a local spring deity in the region. As the Romans often did, they made a hybrid deity, Sulis Minerva. British Sulis was considered a good match for the soldier-goddess Minerva, the deity of war and wisdom. In Bath's holy waters, Sulis Minerva specialized as a protector against disease and misfortune.

One stone relief of Minerva in Bath shows a woman with a thick, woollen robe – handy for West Country winters – with a Minervan head of Medusa on her breast, along with a Celtic face, flame-like hair and a very British, pre-Roman sculptural feel to it. The perfect religious match of Britannia and Roma.

Celtic druids on the Continent were apparently accepted by the Romans, too. Pliny the Elder gives a gripping description of druids who sound just like Getafix in the Asterix books: 'A priest arrayed in white vestments climbs the tree and with a golden sickle cuts down the mistletoe, which is caught in a white cloak.'

Sadly there's no solid archaeological evidence for the presence of Celtic druids in Britain – but Julius Caesar did write, 'It is thought that the doctrine of the druids was invented in Britain.' The druids who gather at Stonehenge every Midsummer's Day are on pretty strong ground, it seems, when they argue they've been around since before the Romans.

Hercules, the Strongman God

Romans literally swore by Hercules. Cicero once invoked Hercules to emphasize that he couldn't take credit for an idea.

Non hercle mihi nisi admonito venisset in mentem.

I wouldn't have thought of it, by Hercules, had I not been reminded.

Cicero, *On the Orator*, 2.180

Hercules (Herakles to the Greeks) was the ultimate hero, the son of Jupiter by Alcmena. His mortal father was Amphitryon, and he lived his life on earth as a mortal, performing 12 labours as a penance for killing his children in a fit of madness. He lived a life of service to his fellow men before dying an agonizing death, thanks to wearing a tunic poisoned by Nessus, a love rival for Hercules's wife Deianira. After his death, Hercules was received into heaven as a god.

As a result of his earlier mortal status, he was the god who understood human suffering best. So he was often invoked in moments of fear or to express strong feelings, as Cicero does – like we say 'Christ!' in moments of stress.

The Romans regarded Hercules as a defender against evil, and Stoic philosophers idealized him for his bravery, endurance and service to mankind.

In time, he was associated with Christian saints for having chosen a life of virtue over one of pleasure – overlooking the hero's healthy appetites for food and sex.

The Augustan poets saw in Hercules a paradigm for Julius Caesar and his adopted son, Octavian/Augustus. They imagined Augustus would join his deified father among the gods. The original intention was that the Pantheon should be a Temple of Augustus. But Augustus knew better, and insisted it should be a cult building named after all the gods, with his own statue appearing in the entrance hall.

The **Pantheon** (Greek for **'Shrine of All the Gods'**) was originally built in 25 BC by Agrippa in the Campus Martius. It was rebuilt with its sublime dome by the Emperor Hadrian in 126 AD. When Hadrian rebuilt the Pantheon, he retained a copy of the original inscription, still there today, above the entrance:

M·AGRIPPA·L·F·COS·TERTIVM·FECIT

which is short for

'M[arcus] Agrippa L[ucii] f[ilius] co[n]s[ul] tertium fecit' – 'Marcus Agrippa, son of Lucius, made [this building] when consul for the third time.'

Agrippa was a Roman general and the son-in-law of Augustus – and his right-hand man. Thus the old joke: whenever Augustus was in trouble, he cried out, 'Get Agrippa.'

The historian Tacitus was sceptical about Tiberius's motives in later refusing a personal cult, and made a telling contrast with his predecessor Augustus. The general view, he said, was that the best mortals *desired* the greatest honours, and so were happy that Hercules and Romulus became gods. But Augustus, they felt, had surpassed them by merely *hoping* for such an outcome:

Melius Augustum qui speraverit.

Augustus, who hoped, was better.

Annals, 4.38.10–11

Today the Pantheon, as restored by Hadrian, stands in the Piazza della Rotonda.

It contains the tomb of the artist Raphael. Instead of a statue, an elegant Latin couplet by his contemporary Pietro Bembo reminds us of his greatness, and shows how accomplished the humanists were in Latin verse:

ILLE HIC EST RAPHAEL TIMVIT QVO SOSPITE VINCI RERVM MAGNA PARENS ET MORIENTE MORI.

Here lies the great Raphael. While he lived, Mother Nature feared being conquered; when he died, she feared she would die.

To get a feel for how the Roman emperors approached religion, gods and the afterlife, consider Hadrian's own words. As well as building Hadrian's Wall, Hadrian wrote a touching farewell to his own soul as he lay on his deathbed in 138 AD.

Animula vagula blandula
Hospes comesque corporis
Quae nunc abibis in loca
Pallidula rigida nudula
Nec ut soles dabis iocos.

Little soul, little wanderer, little charmer,
My body's guest and companion.
To what places will you go now?
Pallid, stiff, naked –
You won't make your usual jokes any more.

Faunus and the Minor Roman Deities

Faunus was one of the many minor divinities worshipped by the Romans. They felt a spiritual force resided in nature, whether in a spring, woodland or open country.

Faunus, associated with herdsmen, shepherds, pastures and woods, was identified by the Romans with the Greek god Pan. As a result, faun was the name given to the goat-legged, half-human creatures, corresponding to the Greek satyrs that accompanied Bacchus and amorously pursued the nymphs in the woods and the hills.

There is a statue of a sleeping satyr, the Barberini Faun, in the Glyptothek in Munich. Carved in the early second century BC, it was found in the Castel Sant'Angelo in Rome and partially restored by the artist Bernini.

Horace asked for the blessing of Faunus as the god passed over his estate in the Sabine countryside.

Faune, Nympharum fugientum amator, per meos finis et aprica rura lenis incedas.

Faunus, who loves the Nymphs and makes them scamper, go gently through my land and sunny fields.

Horace, *Odes*, 3.18.1–3

Horace went on to ask the god not to harm his young flocks and to be kind to his livestock.

Wherever beauty was found in the natural world, the ancient mind saw the presence of the divine. These powers, called **numina** (as in **numinous**), had to be recognized and placated no less than the great gods of Olympus, because they touched everyday life, particularly for those who farmed the land.

The Secular Games and the Moral Principles of Rome

In 17 BC, Augustus held the **Ludi Saeculares** (**Secular Games**), celebrating the arrival of a new age for the Roman people.

Secular didn't mean non-religious, as it does now. The games marked the end of one saeculum – roughly the length of the average lifetime – and the beginning of another. Augustus's games recognized the fifth saeculum of Rome.

As poet laureate, Horace wrote a secular hymn that was sung first on the Palatine and then on the Capitol, by a choir of 27 boys and 27 girls. It shows how certain moral qualities were revered beyond the divine world of the gods.

Iam Fides et Pax et Honos Pudorque priscus et neglecta redire Virtus audet, apparetque beata pleno Copia cornu.

Now Good Faith, Peace and Honour, ancient Modesty and neglected Virtue dare to return, and blessed Plenty appears with a brimming horn.

Horace, *Secular Hymn*, 57–60

The hymn extolled the peace and prosperity enjoyed by Rome, and the return of the old morality of the early Republic, all thanks to the work of Augustus.

Not everyone thought Rome was *that* holy. The satirist Juvenal remarked bitterly that there should be a temple in Rome to **Pecunia** (**Money**), as Romans built temples to everything else but worshipped money most of all.

There was a temple to **Concordia** (**Harmonious Relations**) near the Capitol, on which storks built their nests, making it the noisiest in Rome.

The wilfulness of the goddess **Fortuna** (**Fortune**) was widely known. She was Shakespeare's 'false housewife', looking down from the painted ceiling on to the stage of the Globe Theatre.

As the instrument of procreation, the male member was given divine status and known as **Fortuna Virilis** (**Virile Fortune**), appearing often on cult memorials, particularly where soldiers were based. A guest at Trimalchio's notorious dinner, keen on double entendre, says of someone:

Plane Fortunae filius, in manu illius plumbum aurum fiebat.

He's a real son of Fortune, that one – just had to touch lead and it became gold.

Petronius, *Satyricon*, 43.7

.NAF.

12

Christian Conversion – How Christ Went from Roman Victim to Roman God

The Roman historian Tacitus first mentioned Christ in pagan Latin, proving that Jesus existed.

> **Auctor nominis eius Christus Tiberio imperitante per procuratorem Pontium Pilatum supplicio adfectus erat.**
>
> **The man from whom these people took their name, Christ, had been executed by the Governor of Judaea, Pontius Pilate, when Tiberius was emperor.**
>
> *Annals*, 15.44

Tacitus was writing about how Nero put the blame for the great fire in 64 AD, which destroyed much of Rome, on **Christ's followers** (**Christiani**).

Christians were hated by the people for their supposed **flagitia** (**acts of depravity**). These were thought to include eating human flesh, based on a misunderstanding of Christian communion practice.

Tacitus's friend Pliny the Younger, sent by the Emperor Trajan to govern a province on the southern coast of the Black Sea, wrote in the following letter to the emperor how Christianity was regarded as a capital offence. He examined, under torture, two maidservants who led the worship of the new god. They were called **ministrae** (**deaconesses**) – note the gender of these early ministers of the faith.

Nihil aliud inveni quam superstitionem pravam, immodicam.

I discovered nothing other than a debased sort of cult, carried to excess.

Pliny the Younger, *Letters*

Trajan, in his short reply to this letter, directed Pliny to show mercy to any Christians who genuinely repented of their folly and could prove they worshipped the Roman gods.

Sine auctore vero propositi libelli in nullo crimine locum habere debent; nam et pessimi exempli nec nostri saeculi est.

But if any pamphlets have been circulated anonymously, they should be completely discounted in any accusation. Such a practice would set the worst of examples and has no place in our age.

Trajan, *Pliny the Younger's Letters*

The following inscription on a block of limestone was found in 1961 in the ancient port of Caesarea, on the northern coast of modern Israel. It confirms Pilate's governorship of the Province of Judaea, where Christ spent his life.

CAESARIENSIBVS TIBERIEVM PONTIVS PILATVS PRAEFECTVS IVDAEAE DEDIT

Pontius Pilate, Prefect of Judaea, gave this building in honour of Tiberius to the citizens of Caesarea.

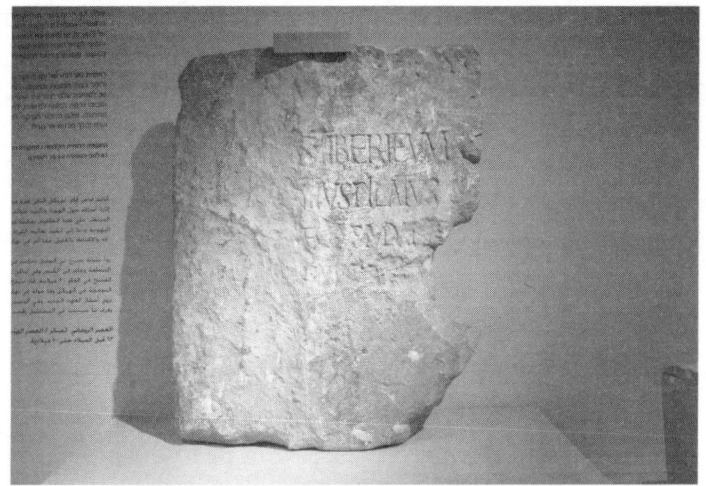

The inscription that proves Pontius Pilate was Governor of Judaea.

A crude representation of a fish was the earliest visual symbol of Christ. It was scratched on walls by early Christians, especially in the catacombs, the burial chambers they used under the city of Rome.

Ichthus, the Greek for fish, was an acrostic for Jesus Christ.

The first letters of the word for fish in Greek (*ichthus*) were an acrostic for the phrase, **Iesous Khristos, Theou Huios, Soter** – Greek for **Jesus Christ, Son of God, Saviour**. This symbol, hastily scratched on a wall, was a statement of faith to others under similar persecution. It was also a reminder of the disciples who fished the waters of Galilee, who were told to be fishers of men.

This early Christian epitaph, from the third century AD, also came from the catacombs in Rome.

DATO BONO SA PARENTES
FILO DATO BENE MERENTI
QVI VIXIT ANNIS XX IN PACE

To Datus their son, Datus the good and well-deserving, who lived for twenty years, his parents dedicated this tomb. May he rest in peace.

The epitaph is flanked by a picture of Christ raising Lazarus from the dead – a popular image reflecting the belief that Christ promised eternal life to the faithful Christian.

This crude drawing was found scratched on the wall of a room in the complex of imperial houses on the Palatine Hill in Rome. It shows a person apparently honouring a crucified man with the head and ears of a donkey.

The crucified Christ is mocked with a horse's head.

The inscription, in Greek, means 'Alexamenos worships his god.' It apparently shows how Romans of the time viewed Christ and his followers as stupid and stubborn. The shame of crucifixion, a punishment reserved for criminals and slaves, is also implied.

In a second-century BC comedy by Plautus, one slave imagined the bloody fate of another, when his bad behaviour comes to their master's attention.

> **O carnuficium cribrum, quod credo fore: ita te forabunt patibulatum per vias stimulis carnufices.**
>
> **You hangmen's sieve, if I know anything about it: they'll stick such holes in you with their prongs, as you make your way through the streets wearing your stretcher.**
>
> Plautus, *Mostellaria*

The quotation shows the process of crucifixion had two stages. First, the criminal was fastened by ropes to a heavy piece of wood, fixed over his shoulders like a yoke (the **patibulum** or **stretcher**). Then he was driven through the streets to a place outside the city gates (to avoid civic pollution), sometimes with whips or **stimuli** (**pointed sticks**), before being hauled up and fastened by nails driven through the ankles on either side of an upright **stipes** (**pole**). The patibulum formed the cross beam of the cross or crux.

The grim torture of crucifixion always appears in Roman comedy in the context of slavery – legally no Roman citizen could be crucified.

This tragic relic of a crucified man is our only evidence for the standard Roman method of execution.

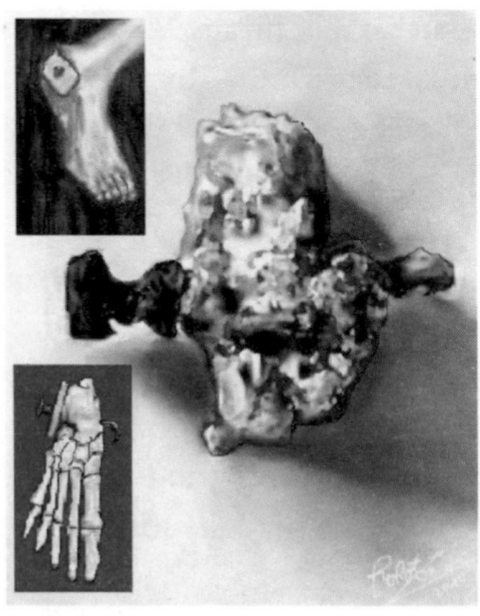

The ankle bone of a man crucified in Israel at the same time as Christ.
The nail goes through either side of the ankle.

It shows that, contrary to later representations in art, victims were nailed through both ankles horizontally on either side of the vertical pole. If nails were used to secure the arms to the patibulum, they would have been driven through the wrists or forearms, not the hands.

The victim on this occasion is known from an inscription to be a Jew called Jehohanan – probably one of the hundreds of his countrymen executed on the hills around Jerusalem, after the Jewish rebellion of 70 AD was crushed by the Emperor Titus.

Pilate, having had Christ flogged, presented him to the crowd in Jerusalem. Pilate's words from this moment are well-known:

Ecce homo.

Here is the man.

Jn, 19.5

According to John 19:19, Pilate wrote on a sign and put it on the cross. The words, meaning **Jesus the Nazarene, King of the Jews**, were written in Hebrew, Latin and

Greek. In Latin, that translates as **Iesus Nazarenus, Rex Iudaeorum**, shortened to INRI.

INRI: Christ by Matthias Grünewald, c. 1510
(National Gallery of Art, Washington).

Pilate's phrase appeared in the Vulgate, the Latin version of the New Testament by St Jerome (347–420 AD), commissioned by Pope Damasus I.

The Old Testament was originally written in Hebrew; the New Testament in Greek. Still, Latin versions became extremely influential. The first known Christian theologian to write in Latin, Tertullian (160–220 AD), claimed to despise the Greek classical tradition that had nurtured his own literary style.

Quid pertinent Athenae ad Hierosolyma?

What has Athens got to do with Jerusalem?

Tertullian's native city of Carthage was a centre of Roman culture and trade. It probably established a Latin-speaking Christian Church before Rome itself.

In his translation of the Acts of the Apostles into Latin, Jerome described the different reactions of the Athenians to Paul's speech attempting to convert them to Christianity. The promise of life after death was a major attraction of the new religion preached by Paul.

Cum audissent autem resurrectionem mortuorum, quidam quidem irridebant, quidam vero dixerunt: 'Audiemus te de hoc iterum.'

When they heard of the resurrection of the dead, some began to mock but some said, 'We shall hear you on this subject again.'

To get a feel for the different versions of the Bible, here is a short passage from the Gospel of John about the wedding at Cana, and the miracle of the conversion of water to wine. The three versions below are the Latin Vulgate, the King James Bible and the original Greek of the New Testament. The words are spoken by the steward at the feast, astonished by the quality of the wine.

Omnis homo primum bonum vinum ponit et cum inebriati fuerint, tunc id, quod deterius est. Tu autem servasti bonum vinum usque adhuc.

Every man at the beginning doth set forth good wine; and when men have well drunk, then that which is worse: but thou hast kept the good wine until now.

Πᾶς ἄνθρωπος πρῶτον τὸν καλὸν οἶνον τίθησιν. καὶ ὅταν μεθυσθῶσιν, τὸν ἐλάσσω. σὺ τετήρηκας τὸν καλὸν οἶνον ἕως ἄρτι

Lots of familiar Latin expressions come from the Vulgate, like this one:

Noli me tangere.

Don't touch me.

Jn, *20.17*

Jesus said these words to Mary Magdalene when she tried to touch him after the resurrection. In the New Testament, it was originally in Greek: Μή μου ἅπτου (*me mou haptou*), which really means something more like 'Stop clinging to me.'

The Vulgate is also the source of these famous words:

Quo vadis?

Where are you going?

Jn, 16.5

Peter asked the risen Jesus this on the Via Appia, as Peter fled crucifixion in Rome. Jesus replied, **'Romam eo iterum crucifigi'** (**'I am going to Rome to be crucified again'**). Thanks to this meeting, Peter turned round and went back to Rome, where he was crucified upside down.

The swords-and-sandals film epic *Quo Vadis* (1951) takes its name from the question. When discussing the original 1896 novel *Quo Vadis*, by Henryk Sienkiewicz, E. V. C. Plumptre, a former classics master, said, 'A classical Roman would have said, "Quo is." What a pity that our Lord spoke such late and inferior Latin.' I'm afraid that Mr Plumptre got things the wrong way round. It was Peter, not Christ, who asked the question.

It's in the Vulgate, too, that this haunting line on the nature of vanity appears.

Vanitas vanitatum, dixit Ecclesiastes; vanitas vanitatum et omnia vanitas.

Vanity of vanities, the preacher said; vanity of vanities, and everything is vanity.

Eccl., 1.2

The spark for the mass conversion to Christianity came in the wake of the conversion of the Emperor Constantine

(272–337 AD). Before the decisive Battle of the Milvian Bridge over his rival Emperor Maxentius in 312 AD, the Emperor Constantine saw these words in the sky beside a vision of Christ's cross – a cross of light above the sun.

In hoc signo vinces.

In this sign, you will win.

After victory in the Battle of the Milvian Bridge, Constantine was confirmed as emperor and declared Christianity the official religion of the Roman empire, ending centuries of Christian persecution.

In fact, those words – '*In hoc signo vinces*' – like Caesar's supposed last words, '*Et tu Brute*', were later Latin translations from the original Greek. What Constantine really saw in his vision were the Greek words 'ἐν τούτῳ νίκα' or, to transliterate, '*en toutoi nika*' – 'Conquer in this sign'.

Even if Constantine's divine message was originally in Greek, though, that didn't stop Latin becoming the official language of the church. Latin was accepted into the liturgy in the papacy of Damasus (360–82 AD), who commissioned Jerome to produce that revised Latin translation of the Bible, the Vulgate.

Constantine's nephew, Julian the Apostate (331–63 AD), was so called because he rejected Christianity. He was disgusted by the venality of the early Christian bishops and reintroduced the worship of the pagan gods. Julian refused to persecute Christians but also refused to encourage the growth of their religion.

Still he was unsuccessful in stemming the Christian tide. He recognized this on his deathbed when, referring to Jesus's home, Galilee, he is supposed to have said:

Vicisti, Galilaee.

You have won, Galilaean.

The decline of Latin came surprisingly late, long after the invasion of the Roman Empire by the Goths and the Vandals in 410 AD. They were surprisingly respectful towards Latin and all things Roman, principally because they too tended to be Christian and respected the language of the church.

At the same time, a Roman elite went on preserving a pure form of Latin well towards the end of the first millennium; like members of Brooks's discussing the correct pronunciation of 'controversy' while the rest of Britain gives in to the alien hordes of *The X Factor*.

Why did the Roman Empire collapse? It's a question that's been puzzling writers ever since Edward Gibbon wrote *The History of the Decline and Fall of the Roman Empire* in the late eighteenth century. One classicist – a German, inevitably – bothered to count up all the various hypotheses for the fall, and came up with 210 of them.

The conventional explanation is the most convincing. In 410 AD, King Alaric and his Visigoths sacked Rome. Across the Empire, from Hadrian's Wall to Africa, legionaries folded their tents and deserted their posts. Several centuries of self-indulgent, over-reaching and in-fighting emperors had done for the whole shooting match, leaving the Eastern Roman Empire to stumble on until the fall of Constantinople in 1453 AD.

The fragmentation of Latin into the vernacular languages of Western Europe – the romance languages – happened with the 'hamletization' of the old empire. Horizons shrank: you no longer had Romans heading off to Northumberland to guard Hadrian's Wall, complain about the weather and the beer, and to spread pure Latin. Travel, correspondence and trade were restricted to the old elites. All those roads that really had led to Rome fell into disrepair or were taken over by bandits.

Thus Latin, once a unitary language constantly garrisoned with renewed supplies of fresh Roman blood, split into a series of lazy dialects. To a great extent, it was the medieval church that maintained pure Latin, while everyday Latin on the streets of the old Roman Empire morphed into Italian.

Consonants got slacker and were lost at the end of words: **Bonus cantat canticum** (**A good one sings a psalm**) became the Italian: '*Buono canta cantico.*' The tricky dipthongs 'ae' and 'au' turned into the easier 'e' and 'o': Latin **causae** (**causes**) became Italian '*cose*' ('things'). All the romance languages lost the genitive, dative and ablative, except for Romanian. They all lost the confusing neuter gender. Latin word order – Subject Object Verb – slipped into the more natural Subject Verb Object, except in Germany.

And so, by the early days of the second millennium, we had what we have now: a series of different languages across Europe, rooted in Latin, but mulched in with pre-Roman languages, all rounded off by the often rather mellifluous shortcuts that come from speaking lazily and colloquially.

There were still several keepers of the flame who kept the pure, old language going. Chief among them was the Church, which sparked the flame when Constantine turned to Christianity at the Battle of Milvian Bridge. Other keepers of the Latin flame include monasteries, the principal hubs of scholarship before the first universities of the twelfth and thirteenth century. Those universities, too, maintained a reverence for old, pure Latin that continued across Europe and in America for another millennium.

It is no coincidence that the last little outposts of pure Latin teaching in this country are grammar schools and public schools: ancient foundations, often of religious and royal origins, that date to a time when Latin was the lingua franca of education.

Today, even as Latin has disappeared from many services, you will see echoes of it throughout the Christian church. And fragments of Christian Latin still filter down the ages. The song '*Ave Maria*' comes from the Latin form of the **Hail Mary** – **Ave Maria** in Latin.

Ave Maria, gratia plena, Dominus tecum. Benedicta tu in mulieribus, et benedictus fructus ventris tui, Jesus.

Hail Mary, full of grace, the Lord is with thee. Blessed Art thou among women, and blessed is the fruit of thy womb, Jesus.

The Eucharistic liturgy in Latin, used by the Catholic church until 1964, is still familiar to many. These sections are particularly memorable:

Dominus vobiscum
Et cum spiritu tuo.

The Lord be with you
And with thy spirit.

In Nomine Patris, et Filii, et Spiritus Sancti.

In the name of the Father, and of the Son, and of the Holy Ghost.

Gloria Patri et Filio et Spiritui Sancto, Sicut erat in principio et nunc et semper et in saecula saeculorum.

Glory be to the Father and to the Son and to the Holy Ghost. As it was in the beginning, is now and ever shall be, world without end.

The Nicene Creed, the defining statement of belief for many Christians, originally in Greek, was decided at the First Council of Nicaea in 325 AD. The Latin translation is more familiar to many Christians.

Credo in unum Deum, Patrem omnipotentem, factorem coeli et terrae, visibilium omnium et invisibilium.

I believe in one God, the Father almighty, maker of heaven and earth, and of all things visible and invisible.

The Lord's Prayer, originally recorded in Greek in different versions in the Gospels of Matthew and Luke, also has a familiar Latin version.

Pater noster, qui es in caelis, sanctificetur nomen tuum. Adveniat regnum tuum. Fiat voluntas tua, sicut in caelo et in terra. Panem nostrum quotidianum da nobis hodie, et dimitte nobis debita nostra sicut et nos dimittimus debitoribus nostris. Et ne nos inducas in tentationem, sed libera nos a malo. Quia tuum est regnum, et potestas, et Gloria, in saecula. Amen.

Our Father, which art in heaven,
Hallowed be thy Name;
Thy kingdom come;
Thy will be done
in earth, as it is in heaven:
Give us this day our daily bread;
And forgive us our trespasses,
as we forgive them that trespass against us;
And lead us not into temptation,
But deliver us from evil;
For thine is the kingdom,

the power, and the glory,
For ever and ever.
Amen.

Latin became the language of the early church, and remains the official language for documents in the Vatican.

The Second Vatican Council (1962–5) allowed languages other than Latin to be used in Mass, but the Tridentine Mass in Latin remains popular, particularly under Pope Benedict XVI, who gave his resignation speech in Latin in 2013.

In 2007, Pope Benedict also made it easier for Catholics to attend the Tridentine Mass, celebrated almost entirely in Latin, and set out by Pope Pius V in 1570. With this masterstroke, the Pope single-handedly ended a battle fought by modernists for 40 years to end the Latin Mass.

The old Latin rite is a splendid sight – the priest celebrates High Mass with his back to the congregation, intoning the Latin liturgy amid puffs of incense, throwing in gobbets of Greek and Hebrew too. Prayers are said at the foot of the altar, matched to a complicated series of genuflections, bows and crossings of the chest.

Although Pope Benedict has quite rightly been celebrated as the driving force behind the Latin revival, his predecessor did his bit, too. In the early 1980s, Pope John Paul II was the first to remove major restrictions on the Latin Mass. In 2001, he accelerated the Vatican's return to Latin when he signed the directive, **Liturgiam Authenticam** (**Authentic Liturgy**), backing translations of the liturgy that are closer to Latin.

The Old Testament may have been written in Hebrew, the New Testament in Greek, but it was in Latin that the medieval priest principally read and in Latin that he spoke in church. It is in the translation from the Latin, too, that worshippers were used to hearing the liturgy.

Confusingly, the Latin Church used a Greek liturgy for several hundred years before adopting Latin, but it was the Latin version that stuck until Vatican II. Still, under Pope John Paul II, it was up to individual bishops whether they allowed the Latin Mass in their diocese. Pope Benedict XVI removed that prerogative from the bishops.

As a result of his apostolic letter in 2007, called **Summorum Pontificum** (**Of the Leading Popes**), issued **Motu Proprio** (**by his own motion**), individual priests could choose to say the Latin Mass. And, what's more, individual congregations could demand that their priest says the Mass.

In 2021, Pope Francis imposed restrictions on the Tridentine Mass in his motu proprio **Traditionis Custodes** (**Guards of Tradition**). But, still, Latin lingers on in the Church, not least in the Requiem Mass for the dead. It gets its name from the introit of the liturgy. Requiem is the accusative of **requies** (**rest**), derived from **re** (**again**) and **quies** (**rest** – as in 'quiet').

> **Requiem aeternam dona eis, Domine: et lux perpetua luceat eis. Te decet hymnus, Deus in Sion: et tibi reddetur votum in Jerusalem: exaudi orationem meam, ad te omnis caro veniet.**
>
> **Rest eternal grant to them, O Lord: and let light perpetual shine upon them. Praise befits you in Zion, O God: and to you is offered prayer in Jerusalem. Hear my prayer, for to you shall all flesh come.**

Other familiar extracts from the Requiem Mass include

> **Requiescat in pace.**
>
> **May he rest in peace.**

Thus the abbreviation RIP on tombstones.

The thirteenth century '*Dies irae*' hymn also appears in the Requiem Mass.

Dies irae, dies illa.

That day, the day of wrath.

'Pie Jesu' (**'O pious Jesus'**) appears at the end of the '*Dies irae*' hymn:

Pie Jesu Domine,
Dona eis requiem.
Pie Jesu Domine,
Dona eis requiem sempiternam.

Pious Lord Jesus,
Give them rest.
Pious Lord Jesus,
Give them everlasting rest.

The most famous version is the '*Pie Jesu*' from Fauré's *Requiem* (1890). Andrew Lloyd Webber's setting of '*Pie Jesu*' in his 1985 *Requiem* was a big hit for his then wife Sarah Brightman and Paul Miles-Kingston, a 13-year-old Winchester schoolboy.

That familiar Christian chant **'Ave verum corpus'** (**'Hail, true body'**) is a Eucharistic chant of a thirteenth-century Italian Franciscan manuscript. The most famous version is Mozart's 1791 *Ave verum corpus* (K. 618), a motet in D major.

That word **Ave** literally means **Be well**, the imperative of the verb **avere – to be well**. It was most famously used in the context of **Ave, Caesar – Hail, Caesar**. Today, Italians still say '*Salve*', meaning 'Hello'. It's directly taken from the Latin **salve – be well**, the imperative of **salvere.**

13

Vesuvius Erupts – Pliny Reports

Two astonishing letters (6.16 and 6.20) about the Vesuvius eruption in 79 AD were written by Pliny the Younger (61–113 AD) to the Roman historian Tacitus.

The 18-year-old Pliny's description of the volcano eruption with its umbrella-like cloud was so precise that, even today, the expression 'Plinian eruption' is used to define the particular instance when columns of hot gases and volcanic debris are blasted high into the stratosphere.

His first letter tells the poignant story of his uncle, Pliny the Elder (23–79 AD), killed in the eruption, aged around 56. Pliny the Elder, also a writer, is best known for the line.

Semper aliquid novi Africam adferre.

Africa always brings something new.

Pliny the Elder, *Historia Naturalis*, 18.31

The second letter describes his observations of the volcano from across the Bay of Naples. For all his precision, though, Pliny doesn't mention either Pompeii or Herculaneum, the towns engulfed by the eruption.

Rather than giving all the Latin, the English translation below has occasional, striking words in Latin, marked in bold.

Extracts from Pliny's first letter about Vesuvius

My uncle was stationed at Misenum [today Miseno, on the northern tip of the Bay of Naples], where he was in active command of the fleet. On the 24th of August [though some people think the manuscript has been wrongly understood and the eruption was actually on 24 October], at about the seventh hour, my mother pointed out to him that a cloud of unusual size and shape had appeared.

He had been in the sun, then had a cold bath, and after eating he was lying around, reading. He asked for his sandals, and climbed to a spot where he could get the best view of that **extraordinary sight** (**miraculum**).

In likeness and shape, the cloud looked more like a pine-tree than anything else. What looked like the trunk was very long and high, and it spread out into several branches because, I think, that while the vapour was fresh, the cloud went upwards, and when the vapour aged, it lost momentum, or was dissipated by its own weight, and spread out to the side. Sometimes, it was **white** (**candida**, which morphed into the English word 'candid'); at other times, it was **dirty** (**sordida**, which morphed into the English word 'sordid') and **spotted** (**maculosa**, as in 'immaculate'), thanks to the earth and cinders rising into the sky.

My uncle ordered a Liburnian [from the east coast of the Adriatic] galley to be got ready. He offered to take me with him, if I wanted to come. I answered that I preferred **to study** (**studere**); by chance, he had given me some writing to do.

He was just leaving the house when he got a message from Rectina, Tascus's wife, who was terrified at the imminent danger. For her villa lay just beneath the mountain, and there was no way out except by ship. So she begged him to save her from such a trap. So he changed his plans, and carried out with the greatest spirit the task, which he had started as a scholarly inquiry.

He had the **galleys** (**quadriremes** - ships with four banks of oars, from **quattuor – four** – and **remus – oar**) launched and went aboard himself, in the hope of helping, not just Rectina, but lots of others, because lots of people lived on the pleasant shore.

Already ashes were falling on the ships, hotter and thicker as they got closer. And pumice stones and black flints, charred and split by the heat, fell too.

[They sailed on to Stabiae]. To calm his friend's fears by showing how calm he was, my uncle ordered servants to carry him to the bath, and, after washing, he sat down and had dinner in very good spirits, or with the appearance of good spirits, which is as impressive as the reality.

Meanwhile, very wide flames and soaring fires were lighting up the sky from several spots on Mount Vesuvius, and the glare and clarity were intensified by the darkness of the night. To calm his companions' fears, my uncle kept saying the locals in their terror had left their fires burning, and that the flames they saw came from the deserted villas.

Then he went for a rest and fell into a very deep sleep. But by now the **courtyard** (**area** in Latin) leading to his room was so full of ash mixed with pumice-stones that if he had delayed any longer in his room, there would have been no escape.

So my uncle was woken up, and came out and joined his friend Pomponianus and the others who had been keeping watch. They discussed whether they should stay under cover or go out in the open. For the buildings were starting to shake with frequent, severe tremors, and seemed to be rocking to and fro as if they had been ripped from their foundations. Outside, the rain of pumice stones, even though they were light and nearly burnt through, was terrifying.

[They then decided to go outside].

They put pillows on their heads and tied them up with cloth, as a precaution against the falling stones. Elsewhere, it was now day, but there it was still night, with a darkness blacker and thicker than any ordinary night. They lifted the gloom with torches and other lights.

My uncle lay down on a sheet that had been spread on the ground, and on this my uncle lay, and he twice asked for **cold water** (**frigidam aquam**), which he downed. Then the flames, and the smell of sulphur which warned them about the imminent flames, roused him and sent the others fleeing.

Leaning on two slaves, he stood up and immediately fell down, because, I think, his breathing was obstructed by the thick fumes and his congested stomach, which was naturally weak and narrow, and often inflamed. When daylight returned – two days after the last daylight he had seen – his body was found intact, uninjured, and covered, dressed just as he had been when he was alive. **The look of his body** (**habitus corporis**) suggested a person who was sleeping rather than dead.

In his second letter about Vesuvius, Pliny described how he stayed at home, reading Livy, when the volcano began to erupt.

Pliny's Second Letter about Vesuvius

For many days before, there had been earth tremors – but that wasn't very scary because it's usual in Campania [still the name of the region that's home to Vesuvius, Pompeii and Naples]. But, on that night, the shocks were so intense that everything round us seemed not only to be dislodged, but falling to the ground.

It was now the first hour of the day, but the light was still **faint and languid** (**dubius et languidus**). The buildings round us were starting to shake. Though we were in an open place, the courtyard was so narrow that there was a great and certain fear it would collapse. So we decided to leave town.

A **stunned crowd** (**vulgus attonitum**, from which we get the words 'vulgar' and 'astonished', ultimately from **tonare – to thunder**, as in 'thunderstruck') followed us. When a crowd is in a panic, it always prefers someone else's plan to its own as the wisest course. This crowd pressed and urged us on in a huge column as we ran away.

We stopped when we got outside the buildings. We then suffered many **miraculous things** (**miranda**, a gerundive, from where we get the girl's name) and many horrors.

For although we were on very flat ground, the **carts** (**vehicula,** as in vehicles) which we had ordered to be brought to us began to sway back and forth, and even though they were wedged in place with stones, they wouldn't stand still on the spot.

Moreover, we saw the sea drawn back upon itself, as if it had been repelled by the earth's tremor. The shore was certainly widened, and many marine animals were stranded on the dry sands (*harenis*, from **harena**, meaning **sand**, from where we get the word arena, because Roman arenas were sandy). On the other side, the black, **horrifying** (**horrenda** – thus horrendous) cloud was torn apart into long stretches of flame, the fiery vapour bursting into long, twisting, zigzag strips. The flames looked like lightning flashes, but bigger.

Not long after, the cloud descended upon the earth, and covered the seas. It encircled Capri [today the popular holiday island] and concealed it. We couldn't see the promontory of Misenum.

Then my mother prayed, encouraged me and ordered me to fly in any way I could. She said that I was young and could escape, while she was old and in bad shape, and would happily die, as long as she knew she wasn't the cause of my death.

I said I wouldn't save myself unless I could save her, too. Then, after clutching her hand, I forced her to hurry up. She reluctantly obeyed, attacking herself for holding me up.

Now the ashes began to fall, but only sparingly. I looked back, and a dense blackness was building up behind us, which flattened itself over the ground and chased after us like a torrent.

'Let's move to the side,' I said, 'while we can still see, rather than being thrown down in the road and trampled on in the darkness by the thronging crowd.'

We were wondering what to do, when night descended upon us – not a moonless or cloudy night, but the sort you see in enclosed places which never see the light. You could hear the **ululation** (**ululatus**) of women, infants' screams, and shouting men. Some were looking for their parents, others their children, others their wives, by calling for them and recognizing them by their voices in return.

Some were **feeling sorry** (**miserabantur**) for their own lot; others for their relations'.

There were some who prayed for death through terror of dying. Many lifted up their hands to the gods, but more were saying that now there were no more gods, and that this night would last for ever.

Others added to the real dangers by inventing new, false terrors. Some of them said part of Misenum was ruined and the rest in flames. Even though this was false, some believed it.

At last, that blackness started to thin, and dissipated into a kind of smoke and cloud. Soon the real light of day came. The sun shone out, but as lurid as it usually is at sunset. Everything had changed in our still trembling eyes and it was all covered with deep ash, like snow.

Returning to Misenum, we tended to our own bodies as well as we could, and passed a **nervous, troubled** (**suspensam, dubiam**) night, in hope and fear.

Pliny the Younger ultimately survived the Vesuvius eruption and lived another 34 years, dying at the age of 52.

14

What Did You Get for Saturnalia? Martial's Funny Festival Presents

In an extraordinary book of epigrams by Martial (*c.* 38–104 AD), he lists the presents at the Roman Saturnalia – the Roman midwinter festival from 17–23 December, which may have influenced the later Christian celebrations at Christmas.

Hosts gave presents 'to be carried away' by their guests. The Greek for 'things to be carried away' is *Apophoreta* – also the name of this book of Martial (also prosaically known as Book XIV). The book lists the poetic couplets Martial wrote to go with these presents, describing the different gifts from rich and poor.

It's so intriguing as an insight into the Saturnalia celebrations – and it's also a rare glimpse at what the Romans really laughed at.

POMADE

Chattic foam inflames German hair: you can be smarter with a captive's hair.

CRINES

Chattica Teutonicos accendit spuma capillos:
Captivis poteris cultior esse comis.

BARBER'S INSTRUMENTS

These weapons are useful for cutting hair; one is ideal for long nails, another for rough chins.

FERRAMENTA TONSORIA

Tondendis haec arma tibi sunt apta capillis;
Unguibus hic longis utilis, illa genis.

A NIGHT-LAMP

I am a night-lamp that witnesses the pleasures of the sofa; do whatever you want – I will be silent.

LUCERNA CUBICULARIS

Dulcis conscia lectuli lucerna,
Quidquid vis facias licet, tacebo.

DUMB-BELLS

Why do strong arms tire themselves out with stupid dumb-bells? It's much better to exercise yourself by digging up vines.

HALTERES

Quid pereunt stulto fortes haltere lacerti?
Exercet melius vinea fossa viros.

TOOTH POWDER

What use am I to you? Please let a young girl use me. I am not used to polishing false teeth.

DENTIFRICIUM

Quid mecum est tibi? me puella sumat:
Emptos non soleo polire dentes.

Of all the Roman writers, Martial was perhaps the most sympathetic – notably in this charming epigram, about the point of life, to his friend Julius Martialis.

If I were allowed, dear Martialis, to enjoy carefree days with you, and to pass my idle hours, and be free for a really full life, we wouldn't waste our time on grand halls or the mansions of tycoons, or grim lawsuits and the miserable forum, or pompous ancestral pictures.

But instead exercise, stories, funny books, the Campus [the Campus Martius, the parks around the Pantheon], the portico, shade, the Aqua Virgo [a viaduct that supplied Rome], the baths – these would be our haunts and the places we 'work'.

These days, neither of us lives our life for our own benefit, and it feels like good, sunny days are slipping away and disappearing – those days which are lost to us, but still count.

Does anyone, once he knows how to live life to the full, hang around waiting?

Si tecum mihi, care Martialis,
securis liceat frui diebus,
si disponere tempus otiosum
et verae pariter vacare vitae:
nec nos atria nec domos potentum
nec litis tetricas forumque triste

nossemus nec imagines superbas;
sed gestatio, fabulae, libelli,
campus, porticus, umbra, Virgo, thermae,
haec essent loca semper, hi labores.
Nunc vivit necuter sibi, bonosque
soles effugere atque abire sentit,
qui nobis pereunt et inputantur.

Quisquam vivere cum sciat, moratur?

15

Horace, the Sweetest Poet of All

Quintus Horatius Flaccus, aka Horace (65–8 BC), is the most quoted Roman lyric poet.

His most famous line is **Carpe diem – Seize the day** – from Horace's *Odes*. It got a second lease of life when it was admiringly quoted by Robin Williams as the inspirational schoolmaster in *Dead Poets Society* (1989). Here are the original Horace lines.

Dum loquimur, fugerit invida aetas:
carpe diem, quam minimum credula postero.

As long as we're talking, hostile time is fleeing: so get a bloody move on, instead of hanging around hoping for something better to turn up.

Odes, 1.11

Of all the Latin poets, Horace is the most sweet and joyous. How would you translate **sweet** and **joyous**? **Dulcis**, I think – such a lovely word. No surprise that it's so popular in Italian, too – think *La Dolce Vita* and *dolcelatte*, that delicious, sweet-milked Italian cheese. Horace used the word a lot – most famously in one of his odes:

Dulce et decorum est pro patria mori.

It is lovely and honourable to die for your country.

Odes, 2.13

Wilfred Owen borrowed the line for his poem, '*Dulce et Decorum Est*':

My friend, you would not tell with such high zest
To children ardent for some desperate glory,
The old Lie: *Dulce et decorum est*
Pro patria mori.

It's funny how often sweet joy – and the word *dulcis* – crops up in Horace's odes – 11 times in the first book alone. And it is used in subtly different ways, shape-shifting to adapt to the noun it accompanies. In Ode 1.13, he writes of **dulcia barbare laedentem oscula** – **'This savage whose kisses bruise that exquisite mouth** which Aphrodite imbues with her quintessential nectar.' In Ode 1.16, he talks about **dulci iuventa, 'the sweet madness of youth** – that drove me in the heat of indignation to dash off that witty lampoon'.

In Ode 1.22, he uses it twice of Lalage:

Dulce ridentem Lalagen amabo,
dulce loquentem.

I'll still love Lalage, my sweet chatterer with the charming smile.

And, in Ode 1.37, he writes of Cleopatra that she is

Fortunaque dulci ebria.

Tipsy with sweet good luck.

And he uses the word in one of his most famous odes, to Thaliarchus, I.IX, when he talks about **dulcis amores**: 'Now that you're young, and peevish grey hairs are distant, don't avoid **the heart's sweet business** or the dance floor.'

That was the ode spoken by the war hero and travel writer Patrick Leigh Fermor beneath Mount Ida, just after he'd kidnapped Karl Heinrich Kreipe, the Nazi general, in Crete in 1944. As they passed Mount Ida, supposedly the birthplace of Zeus, General Kreipe recited the first line of the ode:

Vides ut alta stet nive candidum Soracte.

Look how the snow lies deeply on glittering Mount Soracte.

At this point, Paddy Leigh Fermor recited the rest of the poem, later saying he realized then that he and the German general had 'drunk at the same fountains'.

Paddy Leigh Fermor had exactly the right joyous, sweet, pleasurable approach to Horace and Latin. A recent issue of the *Philhellene*, a lovely magazine devoted to Leigh Fermor, published, for the first time, a Latin translation Paddy did at the school, when he was only 15. And what should he have chosen to translate but Ode I.9, the Ode to Thaliarchus – the ode he would recite on the slopes of Mount Ida to a Nazi general 14 years later?

The translation, in rhyming triplets, is pretty good for a 15-year-old boy. It does have some of the clumsiness of youth:

See, Soracte's mighty peak stands deep in virgin snow,
And soon the heavy-laden trees their white load will not know
When the swiftly rushing rivers with the ice have ceased to flow.

Vides ut alta stet nive candidum
Soracte nec iam sustineant onus
silvae laborantes geluque
flumina constiterint acuto?

It also has some of those classic archaisms and consciously-poetic, over-reverent translations that we all go in for when we're adolescent and trying to sound all highfalutin'.

Now doth a roguish laugh our hiding girl betray
From her dark cover, where love's token, perforce, is snatched away,
And her ill-withstanding finger but feebly bids him nay.

Nunc et latentis proditor intimo
gratus puellae risus ab angulo
pignusque dereptum lacertis
aut digito male pertinaci.

It was only months after his translation appeared in the school magazine, the *Cantuarian*, that Leigh Fermor committed a properly sweet, pleasurable offence – he was caught holding hands with Nelly Lemar, the daughter of a Canterbury greengrocer. There followed what the school called a **consilium abeundi** – a lovely gerund, meaning **an advice to leave**. In other words, he was expelled.

He spent the next 80 years walking across Europe, kidnapping German generals, generally making love to beautiful women, staying in a wide selection of castles and schlosses, writing books, and building the most lovely house in the Mani.

In that time, Paddy Leigh Fermor also perfected the art of bringing joy and sweetness to the reading of Latin in general, and Horace in particular. Over the years, those schoolboy archaisms and that reverence for Latin disappeared, to be replaced by sheer pleasure in the poems and the language.

In *Dashing for the Post*, Leigh Fermor's collected letters, Leigh Fermor wrote in 1980 to Niko Ghika, the Greek painter, about his perfect kind of translation from Latin: 'I think that's a wonderful way to approach Latin – and Horace – as a living language, instead of a stone-dead inscription on blurred and overgrown marble.'

I have in fact heard Horace spoken just like Italian. A few years ago, a Bologna professor at a classics conference, the Festival del Mondo Antico, in Rimini read out Ode 1.37. He wasn't like traditional classics dons – he was tanned a nut-brown, in white pipe-cleaner trousers, a white blouson jacket, the sleeves rolled up to the elbows, his candy-striped shirt ripped open to the navel revealing a wiry chest tanned the colour of brown furniture by the Adriatic sun.

He didn't read Virgil like an English don either. '*Nunc est bibendum*' came out less like a retired optician from Malvern trying to buy stamps in Rome – i.e. English schoolboy pronunciation – and more like romantic, rat-a-tat Italian spoken by a Naples street urchin chatting up Sophia Loren. He spoke Horace just like Italian, *con brio*, and it sounded so much more convincing than the plodding Anglo-Latin I'd been speaking for years.

At my old school, Westminster, we spoke our Latin prayers in a robust English accent. A useful reminder that Julius Caesar was, of course, an Englishman.

And so we would ponderously recite Horace's Odes 1.37 with its famous first three words:

Nunc est bibendum, nunc pede libero
Pulsanda tellus.

Now we must drink; now the earth must be shaken under a wild foot.

This Bologna professor said it quickly and naturally, with real joy and sweetness.

Those words, **Nunc est bibendum – Now we must drink** – have, not surprisingly, become much treasured. Bibendum even lent itself to the name of a popular west London restaurant.

Bibendum is a gerundive, which has the element of obligation, as in Horace's line, **Nil desperandum – Never despair** or, literally, 'It must never be despaired of.' The full line is:

Nil desperandum Teucro duce et auspice Teucro.

No need to despair – with Teucer as your leader and Teucer to protect you

Horace, *Odes*, 1.7.27

Another famous gerundive was declared by Cato the Elder (234–149 BC) when Rome was at war with Carthage. Cato finished every speech in the Senate with these words.

Delenda est Carthago.

Carthage must be destroyed.

Pliny the Elder, *Naturalis Historia*, 15.74

A gerundive also found its way into this bit of cod Latin, popular during the Second World War:

Nil carborundum illegitimi.

Don't let the bastards grind you down.

Another gerundive – **amanda** – means **a woman who ought to be loved**; thus the name Amanda. **Pudenda**, as in genitals, literally means **things to be ashamed of.**

In that Horace ode translated by Leigh Fermor, there's another memorable couplet:

> **Quid sit futurum cras fuge quaerere et**
> **quem fors dierum cumque dabit lucro appone.**
>
> **Don't ask what tomorrow holds in store for you. Call every day that Fortune gives you a bonus.**

It was Horace, too, who most funnily captured the idea of the town mouse and the country mouse, staying in each other's houses. Both of them hated the other's place. The Town Mouse is staying in the sticks with the Country Mouse:

> **Tandem urbanus ad hunc 'quid te iuvat,' inquit,**
> **'Amice, praerupti nemoris patientem vivere dorso?**
> **Vis tu homines urbemque feris praeponere silvis?'**
>
> **At last, the Town Mouse asks, 'What's the point, my friend,**
> **In barely surviving, in this wood on a precipitous ridge?**
> **Wouldn't you prefer the city to these wild forests?'**
>
> *Satires*, 2.6.90–2

Shortly after, the Town Mouse also says to the Country Mouse, **'Carpe viam'**, meaning **'Seize the road'** or 'Come with me'. It's a play on those famous words, also by Horace, *Carpe diem*.

The Country Mouse duly comes to the city for a slap-up feast with the town mouse, only to be chased away by terrifying Molossian hounds – a breed famous in ancient Greece.

Tum rusticus: 'Haud mihi vita

est opus hac,' ait et 'Valeas: me silva cavusque tutus ab insidiis tenui solabitur ervo.'

Then the Country Mouse says, 'This life's no good to me. And so goodbye: my woodland hole and simple vetch, safe from such horrors, will do for me.'

You sense that Horace, too, really preferred the country mouse's life. In one of his Epistles, he declared

Naturam expelles furca, tamen usque recurret et mala perrumpet furtim fastidia victrix.

You might drive out nature with a pitchfork, but she will always rush back and, before you know it, she will smash up and triumph over your silly disapproval of her.

Epp., 1.10.24–5

16

Cicero on How to Grow Old Gracefully

The Roman writers were masters at the art of consolation. Virgil put it beautifully in describing Aeneas trying to lift the spirits of his miserable men when things are going badly in their quest to found Rome. He declares,

> **Forsan et haec olim meminisse iuvabit.**
>
> **One day perhaps it'll cheer us up to remember even these things.**
>
> *Aeneid*, 1.203

How true: looking back at the depths of your misery a few years later gives you a sense of proportion. It can even produce a kind of spirit-booster as you begin to think you can recover from most things.

In the next passage, Cicero (106–43 BC) provides consolation in the face of that perpetual provider of miseries, old age. He wrote the essay – *Cato Maior de Senectute* (*Cato the Elder on Old Age*) – in 44 BC. The essay is written as if it was delivered by Cato the Elder (234–149 BC), a Roman senator and the first historian to write in Latin. The essay is translated into English, with striking phrases added in the original Latin.

What a brilliant reply Sophocles gave when, as an old man, he was asked if he still indulged in sex.

'Heaven forbid!' he said. 'I'm delighted to have escaped **from such a savage and cruel master (ab domino agresti ac furioso profugi)**.'

Lots of people never complain about old age. Instead, like Sophocles, they're delighted at being freed from the chains of desire for pleasure. When others complain about getting old, it's not their age that's the problem. It's their character. Old men who are self-controlled and free of bad temper and boorishness find old age bearable. But if you don't have tact or finer feelings, then every stage of life is a nuisance.

What could be better than a peaceful and gentle old age spent quietly, with integrity and discrimination? Look at Plato. **He died while he was writing, in his eighty-first year** (**uno et octogesimo anno scribens est mortuus**). Or what about Isocrates, the Greek orator? He was 93 when he wrote *Panathenaicus*, about the literacy of the Spartans, and he lived on for another five years.

Gorgias of Leontini, his teacher, lived till 107, without losing enthusiasm for his work. When he was asked why he wanted to stay alive for so long, he said, **'I've got no reason to find fault with old age.' ('Nihil habeo quod accusem senectutem').**

What an outstanding reply! How worthy of a man of letters! (Praeclarum responsum et docto homine dignum). Only idiots attribute to old age their own failings and their own faults.

I couldn't disagree more with Caecilius Statius, the playwright, when he says, **'The most wretched thing in old age is realizing that you're a bore to other people.'**

(Tum equidem in senecta hoc deputo miserrimum, sentire ea aetate eumpse esse odiosum alteri.)

In fact, you can be a delight rather than a bore. Wise old men are delighted by clever young men, and old age is easier if you're cultivated and appreciated by the young. In the same way, young men love being taught by old men how to be more virtuous.

Old age isn't a feeble and idle time. You should be busy, trying to achieve the same sort of things you did when you were younger.

You can always learn something new. The Athenian politician, Solon, said in his poems that he learnt something new every day in old age.

I'm 62 and I'm learning Greek. I love it. I drink it down greedily like I'm satisfying a long-standing thirst. And now I'm familiar with all the Greek writing techniques I'm using in this article.

Socrates learnt how to play the lyre in old age. I'd have loved to have done that, too, **but at least I've been catching up on my ancient Greek literature** (**sed in litteris certe elaboravi**).

I don't long to be strong, like I was when I was young; any more than, when I was young, I longed for the strength of a bull or an elephant. A man should use the strength that he has, and act in accordance with that strength.

What could be more annoying than the remark made by Milo of Croton, the Greek wrestler in the sixth century BC, who was an Olympic champion six times?

When he was an old man, watching the athletes training on the racecourse, he looked at his arms and said, with tears in his eyes, **'Well, these are certainly dead now.' ('At hi quidem mortui iam sunt.')**

They're not as dead as you are, you idiot. It was never your real self that made you famous, but your lungs and your arms.

Give me those law experts, Sextus Aelius, Tiberius Coruncanius and Publius Crassus. They were teaching law to their fellow citizens right up until their last, dying breath.

In old age, somehow or other, the brilliant quality of resonance in a voice actually improves. It hasn't deserted me yet, and you can see how old I am in my statues. What suits an old man best is a quiet, gentle style of speech. When an old man is eloquent, the elegance and mellifluous quality of his voice compel the listeners' attention.

Old age wins honour, as long as it defends itself by its actions, preserves its rights, surrenders to no one else's power and, until its final breath, holds sway over its family.

I thoroughly approve of the old man who keeps something of the young man in his soul; just as much as I approve of the young man with something of the old man in him. Anyone who follows this principle will be old in body, but never in mind.

In the end, what is more natural than for old people to die? **Everything that aligns with nature is right. (Omnia autem quae secundum naturam fiunt sunt habenda in bonis.)**

When young people die, nature fights against the unfairness. It's like a strong flame being extinguished by a torrent. But, when old men die, it's like a fire going out of its own accord, once all the fuel's been used up, without any force being applied.

It's like when you struggle to pluck green apples from trees; while they fall of their own accord if they're ripe and mature. It's force that takes life away from young men; ripeness that takes it away from the old.

This idea of ripeness pleases me so much that, the closer I get to dying, the more I feel like a sailor at sea, who has spotted land and is about to come into harbour after a long voyage. Old age has no fixed end. A man lives out his last years properly if he can still fulfil his duties and have no regard for death. This leads to old age having more spirit than youth, and more courage.

This explains what Solon said when Pisistratus, the tyrant, asked him, 'What is it that makes you so bold in opposing me?'

'Old age' ('Senectute'), Solon said.

17

Seneca's Stoic Guide to Life

The greatest Roman Stoic philosopher was Seneca (4 BC–65 AD).

The Stoics were a Greek school, founded in Athens in the third century BC by Zeno of Citium. But it was Seneca who took Stoic thought to its highest pitch, writing in Latin. Here are Seneca's wisest thoughts on how to tackle life's miseries.

Good men should not be afraid to face hardships and difficulties, or complain of fate. It is not what you endure that matters, but how you endure it.

Scias licet idem uiris bonis esse faciendum, ut dura ac difficilia non reformident nec de fato querantur; non quid sed quemadmodum feras interest.

God does not pamper a good man like a favourite slave; he puts him to the test, hardens him, and makes him ready for His service.

Deus bonum virum in deliciis non habet, experitur indurat, sibi illum parat.

Pain is not an evil.

Non malum dolor.

It is by enduring ills that the mind can acquire contempt for enduring them.

Ad contemnendam patientiam malorum animus patientia pervenit.

No man is crushed by misfortune unless he has first been deceived by prosperity.

Nemo fortuna opprimitur nisi prius prosperitate deceptus est.

Do not fear the name of death. Death is a law of nature, a contribution and an obligation required of mortals, a cure for all ills.

Noli nomen mortis timere; mors est naturae lex, est donum ac officium mortalibus impositum; est omnium malorum remedium.

QVOD OLIM FVIT MEMINISSE MINIME IVVAT

This inscription at Broughton Castle, Oxfordshire – 'It hardly helps to remember what happened in the past' – is a witty play on Aeneas's words in the Aeneid: **Forsan et haec olim meminisse iuvabit – 'Perhaps one day it will help to remember even these things'.**

18

Your Vade Mecum – the Latin-English Glossary

As you'll see further down in this chapter, **Vade mecum** literally means **'Go with me.'** It came to mean something, often a book, you carry with you every day.

Well, here's your ideal vade mecum: a list of the popular – and not so popular – Latin words, phrases and quotations used in English. A literal translation is given, followed by a colloquial one if needed.

Actus reus & **mens rea – Guilty act** & **guilty mind**
Two elements of a crime in law. For murder, for example, you need both: the killing and a criminal intention. Manslaughter would involve the killing, or *actus reus*, without the criminal intention, the *mens rea*.

Adeste fideles – 'O come, all ye faithful!'
The hymn was originally in Latin by an unknown author.

Ad hoc – For this purpose
Temporarily useful or improvised.

Ad hominem/ad rem – To the man/To the thing
Dealing with an individual/dealing with an issue.

Ad infinitum – Until infinite
Indefinitely.

Ad libitum – At pleasure

Off the cuff. Better known as ad lib.

Ad nauseam – Until sickness

Endlessly.

Advocatus diaboli – Devil's advocate

Also known as the **promotor fidei** (**promoter of the faith**). In the Vatican, the devil's advocate argues against a beatification or canonization.

Aegrotat – He is sick

Used for degrees taken by undergraduates who are too ill to do exams.

Aetas parentum peior avis tulit nos nequiores, mox daturos progeniem vitiosiorem.

Our grandfathers sired children who were worse than themselves, and they fathered us, worse still and soon to produce offspring who are even more corrupt.

(Horace, *Odes*, 3.6.46–8)

For all his sweet love poetry, Horace could be a bit of an old fogey, as in the lines above. Boris Johnson once said of him in the *Telegraph*,

> Horace sometimes reads like Melanie Phillips of the *Daily Mail* after a particularly difficult Tube ride. 'Young girls think of sex to the tips of their tender fingers!' 'Is this the race that conquered Antiochus and Hannibal?' asks Simon Heffer. 'I tell you what,' says Peter Hitchens in a provocative personal view, 'Roman wives these days are having it off with Spanish sea captains and travelling salesmen.'

A fortiori – From the stronger side

With greater reason – used to draw a conclusion that is stronger than a previous one: 'If he can pay off his billion-pound gambling debt, a fortiori he can afford to buy me a drink.'

Alias – At another time

Now means 'also known as'.

Alma mater – Nourishing mother

Used of an old university. The Roman expression was used of Ceres, goddess of agriculture, and Cybele, the nature goddess.

Alumnus or alumna – Nursling, foster child

A university graduate.

Amicus curiae – A friend of the court

A professional who isn't party to the litigation but appears in court to give advice.

Anno Domini – In the year of our Lord

Abbreviated to AD.

When you write, say, 2022 AD, the literal translation is 'in the Lord's 2022nd year'. That's why there was never a year zero between 1 BC and 1 AD. You can't say in the Lord's noughth year.

Annuit coeptis – He has favoured our undertakings

From Virgil's *Aeneid*. The line appears on the back of the great seal of the United States, and the back of the dollar bill.

Ante meridiem – Before noon
Post meridiem – After noon

Abbreviated to a.m. and p.m.

Apologia pro vita sua – A defence of his own life

Apologia is Greek for defence, but has morphed into the word apology.

A posteriori – From what comes after

Arguing backwards from experience or investigation. As opposed to **a priori** – **from what comes before**: arguing forwards from first principles.

Arma virumque cano – I sing of arms and the man

The first line of the *Aeneid*. The first four lines of Virgil's epic are:

> **Arma virumque cano, Troiae qui primus ab oris**
> **Italiam, fato profugus, Laviniaque venit**
> **litora, multum ille et terris iactatus et alto**
> **vi superum saevae memorem Iunonis ob iram.**
>
> **I sing of arms and the man who first came from the shores of Troy, destined to be an exile to Italy and the Lavinian beaches, a man much buffeted on land and sea by force of the gods and because of Juno's fierce, never-forgiving anger.**

Ars longa, vita brevis – Art is long, but life is short

A Latin translation of a saying by Hippocrates, responsible for the Hippocratic Oath. The idea was that a doctor needed to learn a lot in a short time. The saying now also means that art can be eternal, while artists are mortal.

Aura popularis – Popular breeze

Or fleeting fame. The expression was used by Cicero of anybody who was the people's favourite for a while.

Ave atque vale – Hail and farewell

On his brother's death, Catullus said,

> **Atque in perpetuum, frater, ave atque vale.**
> **Hello and goodbye for ever, brother.**

Ave Maria – Hail Mary

From Saint Luke's Gospel, where the angel tells the Virgin of the birth of Christ,

> **Ave Maria, gratia plena, Dominus tecum. Benedicta tu in mulieribus, et benedictus fructus ventris tui, Iesus.**
>
> **Sancta Maria, Mater Dei, ora pro nobis peccatoribus, nunc, et in hora mortis nostrae. Amen.**
>
> **Hail Mary, full of grace. The Lord is with thee. Blessed art thou amongst**
>
> **women, and blessed is the fruit of thy womb, Jesus. Holy Mary, Mother of God, pray for us sinners, now and at the hour of our death. Amen.**

Benedictus benedicat – May the blessed one give a blessing

The most popular form of grace before a meal.

Bona fide – In good faith

Bonus – Good

The adjective came to mean a bonus, the noun in English, meaning a positive thing of a boost to your salary.

Boudicca generis regii femina duce neque enim sexum in imperiis discernunt.

They were led by Boadicea, a woman of royal blood – the Britons are indifferent to sex when it comes to royal succession.

Tacitus, *Agricola* – on Boadicea's Revolt in 61 AD against the Romans

It's striking that, then as now, the British were happy to be led by a queen. The idea of being led by an empress would have seemed ludicrous to a Roman.

Caelum crebris imbribus ac nebulis foedum; asperitas frigorum abest

The British sky is obscured by constant rain and cloud, but it never gets really cold

Tacitus, *Agricola* – on the Miserable British Weather

Camera – A room

Still used in law in this sense: an 'in camera' hearing is one held in the judge's private room. We get our word 'camera' from **camera obscura**: the dark room, where images were projected onto a wall through a small hole. In the nineteenth century the idea developed into the photographic camera.

Casus belli – The justification for making war

Caveat – Let him beware

A warning.

Cf. – Abbreviation for confer – compare

Used in a book or article to mean 'look elsewhere'.

Cincinnatus – A retired Roman statesman and farmer, called on to save Rome in 458 BC. In just 16 days, he saved Rome from invaders. He then returned to his farm and picked up his plough. Boris Johnson referred to him in March 2013, talking to a schoolchild in Norwood, saying, 'If, like the Roman leader Cincinnatus, I were to be called from my plough to serve in that office [of Prime Minister], I wouldn't, of course, say no.'

Circus – A circle

Used of the Circus Maximus – 'the biggest circle' – the great racecourse in Rome. Came to be used of round streets, like Oxford Circus, and the circus as in the round big top.

Civis Romanus sum – I am a Roman citizen

The proud expression recalled by Lord Palmerston in 1850 in the Don Pacifico affair. Don Pacifico, a Gibraltar Jew, had had his house damaged by Greeks. Palmerston sent British ships to Athens, saying, 'As the Roman . . . could say, "*Civis Romanus sum*," so also a British subject, in whatever land he may be, shall feel confident that the watchful eye and the strong arm of England will protect him.'

Codex – A manuscript

From **caudex – tree trunk.** The word was used of a book of wooden tablets, with words inscribed into them in wax.

Related book terms:

Folio – Edition. It comes from **folium – leaf** – which morphed into **folium – page**.

Verso – Left-hand page (from **folio verso – the page having been turned**, i.e. the first page you see after turning).

Recto – Right-hand page, from rectus, -a, -um – set straight. So **recto folio** means **with the page set straight.**

Coitus interruptus – From **coitus – a meeting** – and **interruptus – interrupted**.

Conductor – A **contractor** or someone who leads people together. Thus the orchestra conductor.

Corcillum est quod homines facit, cetera quisquilia omnia.

It's brains that make men; everything else is rubbish.

Petronius, *Sat.*, 75

Cornucopia – Horn of plenty

A horn filled with fruit, flowers and corn sheaves.

Corpus iuris – Body of law
A country's collected laws.

Cum laude – With praise
Magna cum laude – with great praise
An American expression for the second best degrees.

Curriculum vitae – The course of your life, as in a CV.

De facto – From deed or in reality.
Often contrasted with **de iure – according to the law.**

De gustibus non est disputandum – There is no disputing about tastes

Dei gratia – By God's grace

Delirium tremens – Trembling delirium
Used of the shakes of alcoholics suffering withdrawal symptoms. Abbreviated to the DTs.

De minimis non curat lex – The law doesn't care about the smallest things

De mortuis nihil nisi bonum – Speak nothing except good about the dead

Deo volente – God willing

De profundis – From the depths
From Psalm 130 – 'Out of the depths have I cried unto thee, O Lord.'

Doctor – A teacher, from **doceo – I teach**
Still used of all those with doctorates, including, most famously, medical doctors. **Medicinae Doctor – Doctor of Medicine** – is abbreviated, particularly in America, to MD.

Domine, dirige nos – Lord, guide us
Motto of the City of London.

Dominus illuminatio mea –The Lord is my light
The motto of Oxford University, which began as a series of theological colleges. The university's motto is taken from the **incipit (beginning)** of Psalm 27.

Dramatis personae – The persons of the drama
A play's cast.

E.g., exempli gratia – For the sake of example
As opposed to **id est, that is** – to expand on your subject.

Ego – I
Came to be used of our self-identity, often pejoratively.

ELIZABETH II D.G.REG.F.D
On British coins, you'll find this inscription, plus the year the coin was minted. The initials are short for **Dei Gratia Regina Fidei Defensatrix**. Altogether, the Latin means **Elizabeth II, by the grace of God, Queen and Defender of the Faith**.

Emeritus – Well-earned or honorary, as in an emeritus professor.

E pluribus unum – One out of many
The motto of the USA, having been formed out of separate states.

Equo ne credite, Teucri. Quidquid id est, timeo Danaos et dona ferentes – Don't trust the horse, Trojans. Whatever it is, I fear Greeks even when they're carrying presents.

Virgil, *Aeneid*, 2.48

Said by the Trojan priest, Laocoön, when he first saw the wooden horse that brought the downfall of Troy.

Ergo – Therefore

Erratum – Mistake
As in the erratum slip in a book.

Et al. – And the other people
Short for et alii.

Etc.
Abbreviation for **et cetera** – **And the other things**.

Et in Arcadia ego – I am even in Arcadia
Arcadia is still a region in the Greek Peloponnese – a rural idyll now, as it was in classical times. The inscription appears on a tombstone in a Poussin picture. It's also the heading of the Oxford chapter in *Brideshead Revisited*.

Ex cathedra – From the chair or with authority
When a pope speaks ex cathedra, he is speaking in his official capacity – ergo infallibly. Cathedra was used of the bishop's throne and, by extension, it led to the word 'cathedral'.

Exeat – Let him go out
Used of a holiday in schools and universities. An exeat was originally granted to a priest allowed out of the monastery for a short period.

Exeunt/Exit – They exit
A stage direction, meaning the characters or character walk/s off stage.

Ex libris – From the books of or **from the library of**
Most often seen on bookplates.

Ex officio – From the office or **by virtue of the office**
So the monarch is ex officio Governor of the Church of England.

Ex post facto – From a thing done afterwards or 'After the fact'

Ex tempore – Of the time or **off the cuff**

Femur – thigh.
Now used of the thigh bone.

Fidus Achates – Aeneas called his best friend, **Faithful Achates.**
Has come to mean a loyal friend.

Floruit – He flourished from **floreo – I flower**
Often abbreviated to fl. and used of writers: Shakespeare fl. 1585–1613.

Focus – Fireplace
As the heart of a house, focus came to mean the centre of attention.

Fons et origo – The fountain and origin
The original source.

Forum – Marketplace
As the most crowded part of a Roman town, it came to mean the place where things are discussed. **Forum conveniens** is still used in law to mean **the convenient place for a case to be heard** – (or **forum non conveniens** of an inconvenient place). Convenient comes from **conveniens** – literally **coming together.**

Functus officio – Finished his duty
The expression is used of judges when they have given judgment and their order has been sealed.

Gallia est omnis divisa in partes tres – Gaul as a whole is divided into three parts
Opening line of Julius Caesar, *De Bello Gallico*

Gratis – For nothing
From *gratia* – thanks (as in grateful).

Habeas corpus – You must have the body
A person must appear in court before he's jailed.

Ibid. – Short for **ibidem, In the same place**
Often used of books in making a reference to the same thing.

In flagrante delicto – In the middle of a burning crime
Most often used of lovers caught mid-act.

Infra dignitatem – Beneath your dignity
Often shortened to infra dig.

In loco parentis – In place of a parent

In medias res – In the middle of things or right at the heart of it.
This is much the same sense that's used in one of the most famous lines from *The Aeneid*.

> **Moriamur et in media arma ruamus – Let us die even as we rush into the middle of battle.**
>
> Virgil, *Aeneid*, 2.354

In memoriam – In memory of

In nomine Patris et Filii et Spiritus Sancti – In the name of the father, the son and the Holy Ghost

Inter alia – Among other things

Interim – In the meantime
An interim judgment in law only deals with part of the case, pending the full final judgment.

In vino veritas – In wine, the truth

In vitro – In glass

As in IVF or In Vitro Fertilization – test-tube babies, rather than those fertilized **in vivo – in a living thing.**

Ipso facto – By the fact itself

The logical conclusion of a statement: 'I love redheads. Ipso facto, I love Rita Hayworth.'

Ius primae noctis – The right of the first night or droit de seigneur

Junior – Younger. The comparative of **iuvenis – young**

Lex Salica – Salic Law

Under Salic Law, women couldn't inherit estates. The Salian Franks lived in north Germany.

Litterae humaniores – More humane letters, or the first two years of the classics course at Oxford.

Locum tenens – Holding a place

Used to mean a temporary position. Shortened to locum, particularly for temporary doctors. A direct translation into French is *lieu-tenant*, as in the military rank.

Locus in quo – Place in which

Used in law to mean **the place where an event took place.** The judge and jury may visit the locus in quo as part of court proceedings.

Magister Artium – Master of Arts

Abbreviated to MA, the degree above a BA, short for **Baccalaureus Artium, Bachelor of Arts**.

Magna Carta – Great Charter

As in the Magna Carta of 1215, in full **Magna Carta Libertatum – the Great Charter of Freedoms**.

Magnificat – It magnifies
Used of a song of praise, from the Virgin Mary's response to the Annunciation:

> **Magnificat anima mea Dominum.**
> **My soul magnifies the Lord.**

Magnum opus – A big work

Major – Greater
Comparative of **magnus – great**. Used of the military rank.

Maximum – From **maximus, greatest**
Superlative of **magnus**.

Mea culpa – My fault

Media – From **medium – the middle**
Came to be used of an intermediary, as in the press or media, passing on news.

Memento mori – Remember to die
Used of objects that remind you of your mortality.

Memorandum – The thing that one is reminded of
Gerundive of **memoro – I remind of**.

Minimum – Very small
Superlative of **parvus – small.**

Minor – Smaller
Comparative of **parvus – small.**

Mirabile dictu! – Wonderful to say!

Modus operandi – A way of working

Modus vivendi – A way of living

Mutatis mutandis – With the things that need to be changed having been changed From **muto – I change**.

Ne plus ultra – No further or the best in its class

Non sequitur – It doesn't follow

Novus ordo seclorum – A new order of the ages
The motto on the back of the dollar bill, implying that a new order was born on the creation of the United States.

Nulla dies sine linea – No day without a line
Said by Pliny the Elder of the Greek painter Apelles, who drew every day. It was a favourite line of Erasmus – and A. N. Wilson.

Nunc dimittis – Now you may leave
From

> **Nunc dimittis servum tuum, Domine.**
>
> **Now you send your servant away, Lord.**

St Luke

Obiit – He died
Abbreviated to ob., as in 'Shakespeare ob. 1616'.

Obiit sine prole – Died without issue
Abbreviated to o.s.p. in genealogy books.

O tempora, o mores – Oh, the times! Oh, the manners!
From Cicero's first speech against Catiline.

Otium et reges prius et beatas perdidit urbes

> **Idleness, before now, has been the downfall of kings and flourishing cities**

Catullus, *Poem* 51, 15–16

Pace – At peace
Or respectfully disagreeing with.

Pari passu – At the same pace

Passim – Everywhere

Paterfamilias – The father of the family

Pax Romana – Roman peace

Peccavi – I have sinned
Said by Sir Charles Napier after taking the province of Sind, India, in 1843 – i.e. 'I have Sind.'

Penis – A tail
Came to be used of the male human 'front tail'.

Per ardua ad astra – Through struggles to the stars
RAF motto, from the motto of the Mulvany family in Rider Haggard's *The People of the Mist* (1894).

Per capita – by the heads
Or per person.

Per impossibile – Assume the impossible

Per se – Through itself
Or in and of itself.

Persona non grata – An unacceptable person

Post hoc ergo propter hoc – After this, therefore because of this

Post mortem – After death
Or an autopsy.

Post partum – After birth

Post scriptum – After having been written

Abbreviated to PS at the end of letters.

Prima facie – At first appearance

Primus inter pares – First among equals

Pro bono publico – For the public good
Abbreviated to pro bono. Viz. pro bono lawyers, who work for nothing.

Pro forma – For form's sake

Pro tanto – For so much. Used in law meaning 'to that extent': say, of partial fulfilment of an obligation.

Pro rata – In proportion

QED, quod erat demonstrandum – The thing that was to be proved

Qua – In the capacity of

Quantum – From **Quantus – how great.** Used in law to mean the amount of damages paid to a successful party. Thus quantum theory – on the motion and interaction of sub-atomic particles.

Quid pro quo – Something for something

Quondam – Former

Quos deus vult perdere prius dementat – Those whom a god wishes to destroy, he first drives mad
Derived from Euripides.

Radio – I gleam or **emit rays**
Thus radio and radiotherapy.

Radius – a staff or rod
Used of the radius of a circle, as in a spoke in a wheel. As in the shorter bone in the forearm.

Rara avis – A rare bird

Taken from Juvenal:

> **Rara avis in terris nigroque simillima cycno.**
>
> **A rare bird in these parts and very similar to a black swan.**
>
> Juvenal, *Satires*

Re – In the matter of

Or concerning.

Reductio ad absurdum – Reduction to absurdity

Res ipsa loquitur – The thing speaks for itself

RIP – Requiescat in pace – May he rest in peace

Rus in urbe – The country in town

A spot in the city that echoes the country. Martial (*Epigrammata*, 12.57) used the expression to refer to the Janiculum Hill, the hill on the edge of the Rome that is still blessed today with lots of parks and gardens.

Senior – Older

Comparative of **senex – old**.

Seq. – The following

Abbreviation for **sequens** and **sequentes**. Often used in notes in books.

Sic – Thus

Often used in English to denote a mistake in a sentence – it was written that way: i.e. wrongly.

Sic transit gloria mundi – Thus passes the glory of the world

Said by Thomas à Kempis, in *De Imitatione Christi*, of the transitory nature of great schemes.

Silent leges enim inter arma – Laws go quiet in wartime
From Cicero's *Pro Milone*.

Si monumentum requiris, circumspice – If you seek a monument, look around you
The inscription on the tomb of Sir Christopher Wren in the crypt of St Paul's Cathedral.

Sine die – Without a day
Or until an unspecified day – used of proceedings that have no set time to end.

Sine qua non – Without which not
Or a crucial condition.

Species – Shape or form.
Came to mean the different species, or forms, of flora and fauna.

Stemmata quid faciunt? What's the good of a family tree?

Juvenal, *Satires*, 8.1

Stet – Let it stand
A mark next to a crossed-out word or sentence showing the writer wants it reinstated.

Sub iudice – Under judgment
A legal term, meaning still before the courts.

Sub poena – Under punishment
A writ summoning someone to come to court, with a specified punishment if they don't. These days written as one word, and also used as a verb.

Sui generis – Of its own kind
Or a one-off.

Tabula rasa – A writing tablet that has been scraped

Or a blank slate.

Te deum – From **Te deum laudamus – We praise you, Lord**

Also called the Ambrosian Hymn, because of St Ambrose (340–397 AD), the Bishop of Milan, devoted to the *Te Deum*.

Terra firma – Firm land

Or dry land.

Trans – On or **to the other side of; across**

As in translate, transfer or transvestite, transexual, transgender or trans.

Ultima Thule – Remote Thule

From Virgil's *Georgics*. Used to mean the end of the world. Thule was considered the northernmost island in the world, a six-day journey beyond the northern tip of Scotland – somewhere around Iceland.

Urbi et orbi – To the city and the world

The Pope's speeches to Rome and the world.

Vade mecum – Go with me

Used of something, often a book, you carry with you every day. Like this one.

Vagina – Sheath, **scabbard** or **husk of grain**

Later came to mean the female body part.

Velis nolis – Whether you like it or don't like it

The origin of willy-nilly.

Versus – Against

Abbreviated to v. or vs. Incidentally, the R, as in R v Brown, stands for Regina – the Queen.

Via – By way of

Vice versa – The change being turned

Or conversely.

Victoria concordia crescit – Victory grows through togetherness

The motto of Arsenal Football Club. Spurs, their north London rivals, have the motto **Audere est facere – To dare is to do**.

Video – I see

Thus used of the television recording device. Television is a hybrid Greek–Latin word: from *telos* (far) in Greek and *video*.

Video meliora proboque, deteriora sequor

> **I see better things and approve of them, and follow the worse course**
>
> Ovid's *Metamorphoses*, 7.20

Vitaque mancipio nulli datur, omnibus usu – Life is given to everyone on lease – to no one as freehold

Lucretius

Viva voce – With live voice

Or an oral test, usually shortened to viva when used of examining someone's degree.

Viz. – Namely

Short for **videre licet – One may see.**

Volenti non fit iniuria – Injury can't be done to a willing person

A Westminster Abbey monument to James William Dodd, a teacher, put up by **his mourning pupils at Westminster School (Discipuli Westmonasterienses)** after he'd taught there **for 34 years (Per triginta quatuor annos)**. As the Roman numerals say, he died in 1818, aged 57. However good a teacher Mr Dodd was, his pupils slipped up here. The Latin for **four** is **quattuor**, not quatuor.

19

Roman Numerals

Roman numerals are much easier than you might think. Though they look tricky, the rules behind them are in fact simpler than Arabic numerals.

First, here's 1 to 10 in Roman numerals.

I II III IV V VI VII VIII IX X

The crucial ones to remember are V – 5 and X – 10. If you want to write a number one less than these, you put a I in front. To add a number to them, you put a I after. So four is IV, six is VI, and seven is VII. Nine is IX, 11 is XI and 12 is XII.

This principle continues right through the higher numbers:

XX is 20. XIX is 19. XXII is 22.

L is 50. C (short for centum) is 100. XCIX is 99. CII is 102.

D is 500. DL is 550. DLII is 552.

M is 1000. MM is 2000. Thus the year 2022 is MMXXII.

And so on – ad infinitum.

Here are the Latin words for the numbers:

1 – unus

2 – duo

3 – tres

4 – quattuor

5 – quinque

6 – sex

7 – septem

8 – octo

9 – novem

10 – decem

11 – undecim (i.e. unus plus decem)

12 – duodecim (duo plus decem)

13 – tredecim

14 – quattuordecim

15 – quindecim

16 – sedecim

17 – septendecim

18 – duodeviginti (literally two from twenty)

19 – undeviginti (one from twenty)

20 – viginti

21 – unus et viginti

22 – duo et viginti

28 – duodetriginta (two short of thirty)

30 – triginta

40 – quadraginta

50 – quinquaginta

60 – sexaginta

70 – septuaginta

80 – octaginta

90 – nonaginta

100 – centum

200 – ducenti

300 – trecenti

500 – quingenti

1000 – mille

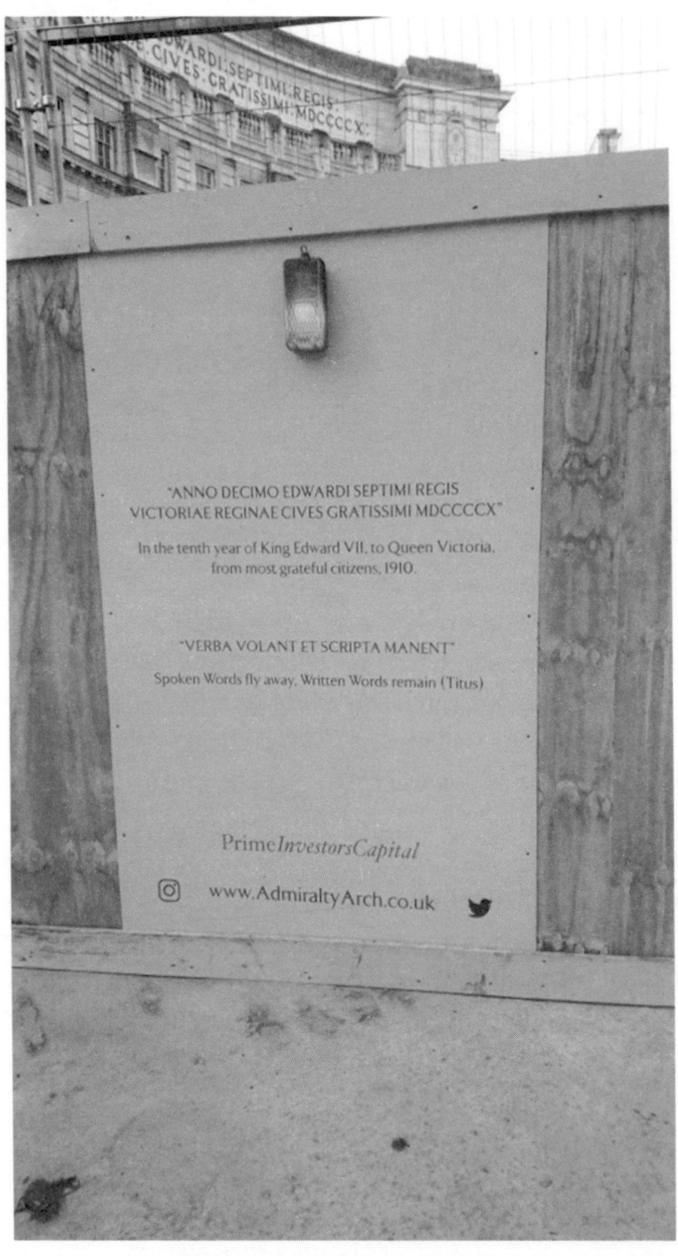

EDWARDI SEPTIMI REGIS
CIVES GRATISSIMI MDCCCCX
"ANNO DECIMO EDWARDI SEPTIMI REGIS
VICTORIAE REGINAE CIVES GRATISSIMI MDCCCCX"
In the tenth year of King Edward VII, to Queen Victoria,
from most grateful citizens, 1910.
"VERBA VOLANT ET SCRIPTA MANENT"
Spoken Words fly away, Written Words remain (Titus)
PrimeInvestorsCapital
www.AdmiraltyArch.co.uk

Modern Latin on a developer's hoarding by Admiralty Arch, London. The first quotation appears on the arch behind. The second quotation comes from Caius Titus, a Roman senator.

CONCLUSION

Is Latin still alive?

Yes, there are some intellectuals like former Pope Benedict XVI who can speak Latin. The Vatican now has a marvellous news programme in Latin, too. What a pleasure it is to listen to the Vatican News in Latin – or *Hebdomada Papae, notitiae vaticanae latine redditae*, to give the broadcast its wonderfully unwieldy, proper name.

The first edition aired in 2019. The announcer, Massimiliano Menichetti, speaks Latin beautifully. His Latin is well-enunciated – so you can hear every word. But he also speaks it fluently and quite quickly, just like a living language. And so you get as close as you can to that impossible dream – hearing Latin as it was said by the ancient Romans.

Menichetti speaks Latin as I've always thought it might be spoken – very like Italian, but with more consonants at the end of words, rubbed down to vowels over the millennia. When you listen to Menichetti read the news in Latin, you're hearing the language that Virgil and Horace spoke, that the terrified inhabitants of Pompeii and Herculaneum yelled as Vesuvius erupted. What a thrill.

Also in 2019, Duolingo, the world's most popular language learning app, launched a Latin version, *Learn Latin from English*.

I'm not suggesting anyone should actually start speaking Latin on the streets of Britain. But it is in treating Latin as a normal language, just like any other, that you begin to recognize its different registers: from the prostitute hawking herself in Pompeii in direct, simple terms to Virgil, writing *The Aeneid* in compact, multi-layered hexameters.

The most recent master of Latin as a spoken language was the American Carmelite priest, Father Reginald Foster. He was the Pope's Latinist for 40 years, from 1969 to 2009. Sadly, he died on Christmas Day, 2020, aged 81.

The Latinist to Paul VI, John Paul I, John Paul II and Benedict XVI, he worked next to the Pope's apartments in the Latin Letters section of the Secretariat of State in the Vatican, previously called Briefs to Princes. Reggie – as he preferred to be called – also taught for 30 years at Rome's Gregorian University and wrote the rigorous, invaluable book, ***Ossa Latinitatis Sola*** – **The Mere Bones of Latin**.

His official duties included translating encyclicals, sentences of excommunication and signposts for Vatican City into Latin. His most enjoyable task was to translate the names of everyday modern words and expressions into Latin. He came up with the Latin used in Vatican cashpoints: **'Inserito scidulam quaeso ut faciundam cognoscas rationem' – 'Insert your card so that the account may be recognized.' Rock 'n' roll** became **tumultuatio**. **Twitter** was **breviloquentia**. **Hamburger with onions** was **bubula hamburgensis cepulis condita**.

In the summer, he ran an intense (and free) Latin course, the **Aestiva Romae Latinitas (Summer Latin in Rome)**. In those lessons, Reggie was a master at picking out charming Latin expressions from 2,000 years ago – including this lovely greeting, from Plautus, the Roman playwright: **Dulciculus Caseus – You Squeezy Little Cheesy**.

Perhaps more than any other Latin expert of the last century, Reggie realized how light, easy, funny and moving Latin can be. His favourite lines included this lesson in love from Ovid's *Ars Amatoria*: 'Drink a little, but not too much.' To show the everyday nature of Latin, even in the imperial court, he quoted the Roman grammarian Fronto's letters to his student Marcus Aurelius, the future emperor: 'I can't teach today. I've stubbed my toe.'

Reggie's lessons were also littered with jokes from the last two millennia.

Take the Roman wit whose graffiti added a tail to the 'D' of **Decus Patriae**, turning it into **Pecus Patriae. The Glory of the Fatherland** became **the Cow of the Fatherland**. To show how literally colloquial Latin was, Reggie shouted affectionately at his pupils in the language: **'Apage nugas!'** (**'Cut the jokes!'**); or **'Expergiscere! Fac sapias!'** (**'Wake up! Wise up!'**).

Sadly, Reggie, his lessons and Vatican News are some of the last vestiges of Latin, as once spoken across much of Europe. Otherwise, it's fair to say spoken Latin is in its death throes.

Written Latin, though, is as vivid and alive as ever – to that admittedly shrinking band of people who can understand the world's most influential language. To read Latin is to bridge the centuries; to connect your mind with the best that's been thought and said. The fundamental reason for reading Latin is because it's the language of Western civilization; because, inscribed in Latin, lie the secrets of our deepest cultural memory.

Latin has inspired the creation of later literature, too. There would have been no Renaissance without Latin. Dante would never have composed his *Divine Comedy* without Latin. There would have been no Milton, Machiavelli or Shakespeare, as we read them today, without Latin.

You also get an understanding of the full, rich meaning of English words with classical origins. With a knowledge of Latin and Greek, two thirds of English words suddenly develop a double meaning – or even a triple or quadruple meaning.

Take 'laundry'. It derives from Old French, which in turn comes from the Latin gerundive, **lavandus** – **needing to be washed**. The same root is found in lavatory and lavish, from the Old French *lavasse*, meaning 'a deluge of rain' – thus the idea of abundance. Today we forget the connection between water, banquets and toilets. But the link is there. Know Latin and you can see the underground roots between them all.

We hope this book has given you a flavour of the deeply buried, extremely thick web of Latin roots that lie below English – and often remain parts of the living English language, completely unchanged over 2,000 years.

There is a Latin expression for every situation – particularly when it comes to ending things. As Augustus said, just before he died,

> **Acta est fabula.**
>
> **The drama has been acted out.**

Everything comes to an end. As Horace put it,

> **Pallida Mors aequo pulsat pede pauperum tabernas regumque turris**
>
> **Pale death smashes his way just as equally into paupers' shops and kings' palaces**
>
> *Odes*, 1.4.13–14

Note that **taberna** originally meant **shop** in Latin before it came to mean a taverna, tavern, bar or restaurant, as it does today.

Horace is the master of the bittersweet farewell:

Eheu fugaces, Postume, Postume, labuntur anni.

Oh, Postumus, Postumus, how the fugitive years slip by!

Odes, 2.14.1–2

Still, Horace can also draw solace from things coming to an end:

Ille potens sui laetusque deget, cui licet in diem dixisse, 'vixi'.

A man will live happily and be in control of his life if he can say at the end of every day, 'I have lived.'

Odes, 3.29.41–3

And, in his greatest lines on death, Horace wrote,

Non omnis moriar, multaque pars mei vitabit Libitinam.

I shall not altogether die, and a big part of me will cheat the goddess of the grave.

Odes, 3.30.6–7

One thing that will never die is the Latin language. As Horace, again, put it:

Exegi monumentum aere perennius.

I've built a monument more lasting than bronze.

Odes, 3.30

We do hope some of those Roman monuments – the greatest Latin lines – will live on in your mind. As Virgil wrote in the *Eclogues*, in a line Father Reggie Foster used to finish his lessons:

Claudite iam rivos, pueri; sat prata biberunt.

Close up the sluices now, boys; the meadows have drunk enough.

Virgil was really saying, 'Now stop your singing, shepherds. You've had your fun.'

And so it is time to write the last Latin word in this book. As Winston Churchill wrote in the visitors' book at Chequers when he finally stopped being Prime Minister, aged 80, in 1955:

FINIS – or **THE END**.

ACKNOWLEDGEMENTS

With many thanks to Robin Baird-Smith, Alice Cockerell, Graham Coster, Daisy Dunn, Shomit Dutta, Peter Ireland, Sarah Jones, Michael Keulemans, Gill Markham, Charles Moore, James Pembroke, John Pickford, Katie Walker (particularly for her advice on Father Reggie Foster), Justin Warshaw, A. N. Wilson and Christopher Woodward.

With thanks to Oxford World's Classics for permission to print extracts from John Davie's translations of Seneca, Horace and Cicero.

With thanks to the Horatian Society, the Patrick Leigh Fermor estate and the Philhellene magazine for his translation of the Horace ode. Many thanks to the *Spectator* magazine for permission to print an extract from Charles Moore's article. Deepest thanks to the *Daily Mail*, *Spectator*, *Catholic Herald*, *Literary Review*, the *Financial Times* and the *Daily Telegraph* for permission to quote from articles by Harry Mount.

Deepest thanks to Philip and Catherine Mould of the Philip Mould Gallery for permission to reprint the portraits of Edward VI and William Arundell.

Many thanks to the following cartoonists for their extremely funny cartoons, which first appeared in the *Oldie* magazine: Ed McLachlan, Nick Downes, Paul Shadbolt, Nick Hobart and Bill Proud. We're very grateful to Rachel Calder and the estate of Ronald Searle for the sublime cover picture from *How to be Topp* by Geoffrey Willans and Ronald Searle (Max Parrish, 1954), starring the immortal Molesworth.

Every effort has been made to contact copyright owners. If there are any omissions, the authors and publishers would be delighted to hear from copyright owners.

PICTURE CREDITS

The following images are reproduced by kind permission of the copyright holders.

Page 5: Edward VI © Philip Mould Gallery

Page 6: Arundell © Philip Mould Gallery

Page 24: The Monty Python Guide to Latin Graffiti © HandMade Films

Page 32: Roman Britannia. From 1911 Encyclopædia Britannica © Public domain, via Wikimedia Commons

Page 37: Londinio Mogontio © Public domain, via Wikimedia Commons

Page 46: The Monument, London © Harry Mount

Page 48: A fresco in the Lupanar, Pompeii's brothel © WolfgangRieger, Public domain, via Wikimedia Commons

Page 60: The Sappho fresco © Naples National Archaeological Museum, Public domain, via Wikimedia Commons

Page 72: Horatius at the Bridge © Ed McLachlan

Page 78: Flora, Goddess of Flowers © ArchaiOptix, CC BY-SA 4.0 <https://creativecommons.org/licenses/by-sa/4.0>, via Wikimedia Commons

Page 100: I suspect match-fixing here © Ed McLachlan

Page 103: What are you staring at? © Paul Shadbolt

Page 114: I Am Spartacus © Ed McLachlan

Page 123: For my next slaying © Nick Downes

Page 124: Before we start © Bill Proud

Page 128: The Roman Empire in 125 AD © Andrei nacu, Public domain, via Wikimedia Commons

Page 132: The five orders of architecture © Vignola, 1507–1573; Juglaris, Tommaso; Locke, Warren S, No restrictions, via Wikimedia Commons

Page 150: A copy of London's earliest inscribed monument © Harry Mount

Page 184: Christians vs Lions © Andy McKay (NAF)

Page 187: Pontius Pilate inscription © BRBurton, CC0, via Wikimedia Commons

Page 187: Ichthus © User:Mufunyo, CC BY-SA 3.0 <https://creativecommons.org/licenses/by-sa/3.0>, via Wikimedia Commons

Page 188: The crucified Christ © Unknown author, Public domain, via Wikimedia Commons

Page 190: The ankle bone of a man crucified © Rubén Betanzo S., Public domain, via Wikimedia Commons

Page 191: INRI: Christ by Matthias Grünewald, c. 1510 (National Gallery of Art, Washington) © Advance at Dutch Wikipedia, Public domain, via Wikimedia Commons

Page 228: The inscription at Broughton Castle, Oxfordshire © Christopher Woodward

Page 250: A Westminster Abbey monument © Harry Mount

Page 254: Modern Latin on a developer's hoarding © Harry Mount